Developing Safer Schools and Communities for Our Children

Developing Safer Schools and Communities for Our Children

The Interdisciplinary Responsibility of Our Time

Betsy Gunzelmann

ROWMAN & LITTLEFIELD
Lanham • Boulder • New York • London

Published by Rowman & Littlefield
A wholly owned subsidiary of The Rowman & Littlefield Publishing Group, Inc.
4501 Forbes Boulevard, Suite 200, Lanham, Maryland 20706
www.rowman.com

Unit A, Whitacre Mews, 26-34 Stannery Street, London SE11 4AB

British Library Cataloguing in Publication Information Available

Library of Congress Cataloging-in-Publication Data

Library of Congress Cataloging-in-Publication Data Available
ISBN 978-1-4758-0753-0 (cloth) -- ISBN 978-1-4758-0754-7 (pbk.) -- ISBN 978-1-4758-0755-4 (electronic)

To the Parents, School Personnel and First Responders that do so much to help our schools and communities.

Contents

Acknowledgments

The following students from Southern New Hampshire University were instrumental in assisting with the research for *Developing Safer Schools and Communities for Our Children*: Megan Klok, Skye Maguire, Laura Towne, and Alyssa Morin.

Writing about the safety concerns that impact our youth was at time emotionally challenging due to the nature of recalling some of the horrific incidents that have occurred over the last many years. However, this turmoil also served as a driving force and demonstrated the need to get the messages out to the public that we can do better making our schools and communities safer for our children and for us all.

A special appreciation is extended to Tom Koerner, Vice President of Rowman & Littlefield Education, for his continued support of my research and writing. Furthermore, the entire team at R & L Education that has worked on the production of this manuscript is commended for their outstanding effort including Christopher Basso for his tireless production work and Carlie Wall for her creativity and expertise in making this work come to fruition.

I applaud the schools and communities that participated in the gathering of information on the parent fears, the educator's concerns, and the issues that abound within their community. I hope through reading this manuscript they will know that they are not alone, their concerns are being heard, and that there is hope.

A warm thank you is extended to all those at Southern New Hampshire University who have supported my work over the years and who continue to do so. SNHU provides a climate of affirmation that stimulates the need to do more for others and I hope I am able to do that through my writing. Dr. Paul LeBlanc, President of SNHU, Dr. Patty Lynott, Provost and Dr. Karen Erickson, Dean of the School of Arts and Sciences all have played a significant role in inspiring my work.

I also am indebted to the following students from Southern New Hampshire University were instrumental in assisting with the research for *Developing Safer schools and Communities for Our Children*: Alexa Grande, Jasmine Hutchins, Meghan Klok, Rebekah Legaspi, Skye Maguire, Alyssa Morin, and Laura Towne.

Introduction

Our world is different than a mere decade or two ago; thus, our communities and our schools reflect the many changes that have occurred. We are more conscious of the needs of others within our local and national communities, as well as the often differing plights of our global neighbors.

Safety problems are more acute worldwide; some involve acts of terrorism, famine, suicide, genocide, and poverty. Others may include health concerns, psychological problems of individuals, and issues that pervade a culture of violence within our society. Although the main focus of this book is on the schools and communities within the United States, it is important to understand that we do not exist in a vacuum. What happens abroad impacts us all.

All children should feel safe and secure within their schools and communities. We have the knowledge and capability to help other children in need, which in the long run helps us all. All children deserve to feel secure, to be nurtured in a safe environment that produces healthy, more humane outlooks toward the global society of which we are all a part.

All this said, it is important to not develop within our children a minidset of paranoia, insecurity, or helplessness. We are not victims. There is much we can do individually and together; our world safety issues have new twists, but really have been issues for as long as mankind has existed. The difference now is that through an interdisciplinary understanding, we can improve the safety of our children and hopefully prevent pointless, preventable tragedy.

All the possible safety concerns are not contained within this book, nor are all the possible solutions. Our world is a rapidly changing place with new problems arising constantly. Flexibility and ongoing research are key to maintaining a safe environment for our precious children.

It is impossible to protect every child from every dangerous situation, but together we can do much to improve and develop safer climates for all children. Indeed, it is the interdisciplinary responsibility of our time.

The following students from Southern New Hampshire University were instrumental in assisting with the research for *Developing Safer schools and Communities for Our Children*: Alexa Grande, Jasmine Hutchins, Meghan Klok, Rebekah Legaspi, Skye Maguire, Alyssa Morin, and Laura Towne.

(Note: the views expressed within this book may not reflect the perspectives of all students.)

Part I

The Critical Need for Safer Schools and Communities for Our Children

There is hardly a day that goes by that we do not hear of some disaster, horrific deed, or other safety concern impacting our children. The need is critical to be able to identify, understand, and hopefully prevent more tragedies from befalling our schools and communities.

The first part of the book helps the reader to grasp this acute need, along with the interdisciplinary nature of the concerns and the manner in which the reported research has been gathered.

Chapter 1

The Critical Need for Safer Climates for Children

The twentieth century will be remembered as a century marked by violence. It burdens us with its legacy of mass destruction, of violence inflicted on a scale never seen and never possible before in human history.

Less visible, but even more widespread, is the legacy of day-to-day, individual suffering. It is the pain of children who are abused by people who should protect them, women injured or humiliated by violent partners, elderly persons maltreated by their caregivers, youths who are bullied by other youths, and people of all ages who inflict violence on themselves. This suffering – and there are many more examples that I could give – is a legacy that reproduces itself, as new generations learn from the violence of generations past, as victims learn from victimizers, and as the social conditions that nurture violence are allowed to continue. No country, no city, no community is immune. But neither are we powerless against it.

—Nelson Mandela[1]

One can hardly pick up a newspaper or turn on the television or other media information device without becoming horrified with the safety problems our children are confronted with on a daily basis. Some involve large-scale tragic events such as the Boston Marathon bombings or the school massacre in Newtown, CT. Others involve individual children being abducted by strangers or even by an estranged parent or relative.

Unfortunately, tragedies have happened; regrettably, we will not be able to prevent every mishap from occurring. But the focus in this book is to help protect children by identifying threats that are currently less recognizable, understanding the complexity of the threatening situations, helping people not to jump to unwarranted conclusions, and assisting with determining the most effective preventative measures and interventions for varying situations and locations. A one-size-fits-all solution does not exist when it comes to the safety of our youth.

The safety issues differ from community to community and from country to country. Our global society's youth suffer such problems as the shooting of the young girl from Pakistan attempting to obtain an education, and that youth from India have the highest suicide rate in the world. Uncontrollable natural disasters including tsunamis, earthquakes, hurricanes, tornadoes, flooding, wildfires, and the like are serious concerns for all, particularly when most schools and communities do not have adequate shelters.

Furthermore, my research on global voices/global visions conducted over the last several years identified a very concerning theme involving a culture of violence that seems to infiltrate many countries. This theme and its associated safety problems is, without a doubt, a global crisis. Although the data vary from country to country on the types and degrees of such problems, all negatively impact our youth hindering their psychological, cognitive, social, and physical development. Our young people are at serious risk, and it is up to us to provide them with the safe and healthy environments in which to grow, learn, and flourish.

In most instances, these dangers are distinctly counter to societies' values, yet they have an insidious way of permeating the very fabric of people, as we have clearly seen in the deplorable events in several communities in the United States. When a tragedy occurs, it impacts not only the victims and their families, but it shocks and paralyzes the communities creating fear, anxiety, and in some a sense of hopelessness; these are all counterproductive to healthy development.

In addition to my current research on global issues, much of my previous research has identified "hidden dangers" that not only create barriers to learning, but also may put our children at risk. For example, some of our current policies may actually unintentionally reinforce an unsafe environment for our children. I believe these practices are contributing to the crisis that includes school violence, students being unable to attain basic skills, students feeling unsafe, behavioral and emotional problems, and other serious health issues. After the Columbine shootings and September 11, 2001, there was a dramatic increase in cases of posttraumatic stress disorder and other anxiety disorders, as well as an increase in cases of depression in children. This unfortunate trend has not declined.

Then there is the unfortunate misinterpretation and fear associated with children who are a bit different than others and have a diagnosis that puts them at risk for being misunderstood, marginalized, and bullied. These children, too, are victims of a form of misdirected, uninformed panic resulting from a culture of violence.

There also are many other types of violence and safety concerns that seem to occur under the radar, or at the very least are not adequately addressed. For example, bullying and cyberbullying are occurring internationally with children even as young as elementary school age.

> Bullying is a widespread phenomenon that involves tormenting victims through various means, including all types of harassment, assault, and attempts to manipulate or coerce victims. It can take several destructive forms, including verbal, physical, sexual, racial, and emotional. One of the more recent developments involves cyberbullying, which occurs through e-mail, instant messaging, cell phones, text messaging, and other technological approaches. Cyberbullying can be severely harmful, reaching the victim in the shelter of his or her home, and it instantaneously spreads the vicious messages to untold numbers across the Internet. (Gunzelmann, 2012, p. 87)

Further complicating the safety concerns, children who are bullied often suffer from anxiety, depression, and lowered self-esteem. Over time, victims of bullying may withdraw and feel hopeless and/or they may become angry and act out, resulting in further violence. We must realize that:

> Bullying is not a normal part of childhood behavior. It is learned behavior and has become deeply ingrained in many school cultures. But what our children need to learn is to respect, understand, and appreciate individual differences and diversity, not to shun or bully classmates for their uniqueness. (Gunzelmann, 2012, p. 88)

Even curriculum choices and delivery approaches may exacerbate safety concerns in our schools.

> Children are impressionable; we all know this fact. We also know that it is more difficult to keep children interested in the classroom today than it was [thirty] and [forty] years ago. Today's children are used to technology with all its special effects; they can easily become bored with the curriculum. In an attempt to make the classroom an interesting place, many teachers resort to curriculum that is definitely sensation seeking but may be contributing to

problems for our children. I'm referring to programs of study that include the darker side of children's literature, where violence and suicide are not uncommon themes; to science lectures that focus more on the "guts and gore" than on understanding the process; and even to history lessons that use Hollywood-version movies about wars, all in an attempt to entertain the children. Unfortunately, they are learning lessons that teachers never meant to teach, and as a result, our children are at more emotional risk. We may be contributing to children's increasing rate of anxiety, depression, and even violence. (Gunzelmann, 2012, pp. 89–90)

How we respond to developing safety policies also needs careful review. Take, for example, the many schools that have adopted zero-tolerance policies, particularly concerning weapons, drugs, and alcohol. On paper, such policies may appear to protect our children, but in reality, they can be quite harmful and at times may even increase the risk to children. The American Psychological Association's Task Force on Zero Tolerance (2006) reviewed research over a ten year period and determined that such policies have not demonstrated that they increase school safety, may actually increase student anxiety, exacerbated issues related to minority concerns, and actually are counter to research from child development experts. Students miss critical time from learning and impact all students, families and the entire community. (Skiba, Reynolds, Graham, Sheras, Close Conoley, & Garcia-Vazquez, 2006). Unfortunately, many such policies have increased youth wariness in authority figures, further undermining safety, and have also unfairly discriminated against minority populations.

Furthermore, little is known on how to intervene with large-scale tragedies, which can be made even more intense by the media. Children can be and have been traumatized by situations of violence, threats upon safety, and uncontrollable events such as natural disasters, as well as the overly dramatized intensity that is now possible with technological advances, but there is limited research on how to work best with these troubled children. It is so important for children to learn to be careful, but not fearful.

Technological developments have brought tremendous societal benefits and basically are neutral tools, but unfortunately can be used in ways that increase the culture of violence, the desensitization of violence, and even violent behavior in susceptible individuals. But we must understand that it is not just a few vulnerable children that are impacted; indeed, each and every one of us becomes anesthetized by violence in the media, video games, movies, and even the daily news. We do know that from the ground-breaking classical research of Albert Bandura (1965) and many social-cognitive researchers that humans and animals are capable of vicarious learning, or learning by observing others. Thus, the models presented in some children's literature, movies, video games, and so on are clearly not the ones that we want our children modeling.

Although we have all heard arguments that not all children will perform such undesirable behaviors, under certain circumstances and with the right consequences, some children will perform them. Even one child is too many. Furthermore, all children who were exposed to such models have learned the behavior whether they act on it or not.

The need is great to comprehend the problems involved that put children at risk. They are complex and at times even perplexing. Some concerns may be more easily remedied than others; all will require a thorough understanding and a deep commitment from all concerned. Nonetheless, our children are at risk and we must protect them.

Developing a safer climate for our children is indeed the interdisciplinary responsibility of our time. It will necessitate research from many interrelated fields with collaboration and cooperation between agencies, institutions, and all involved with children. There is no time to waste, so let us begin.

NOTE

1. (Nelson Mandela, 2002, p.v.) World report on violence and health: summary. Geneva, World Health Organization, 2002.

Chapter 2

The Interdisciplinary Necessity and Obligation

No man should bring children into the world who is unwilling to persevere to
the end in their nature and education. [1]
–Plato

The need and obligation we all share to protect and educate our children
cannot come from just one perspective. We cannot place the sole responsibility upon any one person or group. It is the obligation of all parents, teachers,
community members, local and national leaders, law enforcement officials,

and emergency responders, indeed all civic-minded adults, to take up the charge of making our environment safer for all children. Furthermore, the research from any one discipline is insufficient without the integration of research from many related fields.

We all have an ethical and social responsibility to educate and protect our children from the negative effects within our local and global communities. It is an age-old and global struggle trying to develop a safety net to protect our children. There is much debate on how we should accomplish these goals, although most agree that education is fundamental. However, education with research-based evidence from interdisciplinary fields including (but not limited to) psychology, sociology, economics, political science, neurocognitive studies, public health, medicine, and sociological perspectives is needed to fully grasp the underlying issues.

If we look back through history, we recognize that raising ethical and socially responsible youth has been an ongoing value. This fact has been understood, but not well implemented. Take for example these insightful words:

> [I]f you ask what is the good of education in general, the answer is easy; that education makes good men, and that good men act nobly. (Plato)[2]

The critical task is identifying the problems that exist (within our current and future communities) and determining the best ways to manage concerns through a research-based understanding and implementation with regular feedback and follow-up required for our ever-changing world.

For example, we have a responsibility to make sure that our children are exposed to healthy models whenever possible and to take the time to help children process and fully understand the situations when they inevitably come across harmful models in the news and their everyday lives. Plato's message from eons ago still comes through loud and clear; it is our responsibility to raise ethical and socially responsible children, and it is through a strong interdisciplinary education that we can accomplish this duty.

Georg Wilhelm Friedrich Hegel also understood that education was the key to developing socially responsible youth. He championed: "Education is the art of making a man ethical." He was clear that it is not enough to work toward excellence without embracing the obligation we each have toward others and communities.

A strong focus must be placed on identifying and preventing future crises, global engagement, and social responsibility. Yes, education is indispensable, but how we impart this knowledge effectively is less well understood.

My research focuses on the violence and safety issues within our global society that impact youth. Problems involve school shootings; youth suicide; racial, gender, and socioeconomic differences; and even natural disasters that breed violence and safety concerns. Such recent dreadful happenings in Newtown, CT, the shooting of the young girl from Pakistan attempting to obtain an education, and youth from India with the highest suicide rate in the world are leading illustrations of such worldwide atrocities.

The culture of violence theme and associated safety problems have created, without a doubt, a global crisis. Although the data vary from country to country on the types and degrees of such problems, all negatively impact our youth hindering their psychological, cognitive, social and physical development. Our young people are at serious risk and it is up to us to provide them with the safe and healthy environments in which to grow, learn and flourish.

How we *respond to developing safety policies* also needs careful review. Take for example the many schools that have adopted zero-tolerance policies, particularly concerning weapons, drugs, and alcohol. On paper such policies may appear to protect our children, but in reality, they can be quite harmful and at times may even increase the risk to children. The American Psychological Association's Zero Tolerance Task Force reviewed research on the effects of zero-tolerance policies over a 10-year period and determined that such policies have not made schools safer places, but actually increased problems including dropout rates! Unfortunately many such policies have increased youth wariness in authority figures further undermining safety and also unfairly discriminated against minority populations.

(We must keep in mind that for all the good the media does by keeping us informed, and allowing for quick, sometimes life-saving communication, there, too are negative impacts that must be mitigated with the broadcasting advances.) Such natural disasters as tsunamis, hurricanes, earthquakes, and tornadoes have tremendous impact on children through the potential loss of family members, friends, and pets; loss of home and belongings; and community upheaval. When tragedies such as September 11, war, and domestic violence occur, the impact is potentially increased due to the deliberate nature of these acts. When children experience, or in many cases even are witness to violence within families, communities, and society, serious psychological harm can occur including PTSD (Post Traumatic Stress Disorder) and other serious and life-altering anxiety disorders and depression.

The questions remain: can we identify children at risk for violent outbursts, while protecting those with psychological diagnoses (most of whom are not dangerous) from being misidentified and victimized? Can we prevent such eruptions from occurring, thus helping not only the potential offender, but also protecting potential victims? Can we identify the factors that are contributing to violence in our world, while protecting the potential good that has and can be realized through technological advances? Can we make the needed changes within our society, communities, and schools to ensure a safer place for all to learn, to grow and live?

The significance of this research is profound: our youth are the future of our communities and our global society. Thus, through global and community engagement and focused social responsibility the implication for this work has the potential to bring our communities together through a shared bond to protect all youth. The result may open channels of collaboration, cooperation and a better understanding of our fellow man.

It is time we understand this developing culture of violence and safety problems impacting our youth. Identification and understanding of the complexity of these problems is a critical first step to developing effective, research-based prevention and intervention strategies. Clearly, as our communities develop, science and technology advances, and our world changes, there is a critical need for collaboration and cooperation through communication summits and ongoing research through the institute.

Through this research and teamwork, we hope to be able to develop effective approaches to increase childhood safety. Certainly education will be a strong part of the development of successful interventions, but it will require the integrated efforts from many fields. Public health, psychology, sociology, and the medical fields are critical keys to help education impart the synthesized knowledge and help pave the way for our policy makers to build a safer reality for us all.

NOTES

1. Retrieved 12/14/15 from www.brainyquote.com/quotes/quotes/p/plato397319.html

2. In Boeree, 2006. p.22/ 71. (Although Plato may not have been politically correct, since women were not as educated as men in his time in history, I include women, as well in this understanding of education.)

Chapter 3

The Crucial Research

Children are the world's most valuable resource and its best hope for the future.
–John F. Kennedy[1]

A background in education, as well as other experiences, have led to the safety concerns of children being at the forefront of my research and writing. One such instance occurred in some earlier schooling when safety was violated within my high school for a very short period of time.

This was back in the 1960s when bussing was in its prime in a Boston suburb. It has always been and still is important that all children need to have access to the best schools. The students being bussed in from Roxbury (a section of Boston), were unsure of what to expect upon their arrival. Such feelings of uncertainty can intensify concerns over safety. This particular group brought with them their friends armed with switchblades for protection.

It was impressive the way the administrators at this public high school managed the situation, all without violence and with respect for the feelings and needs of each student and teacher within this community. The students were not allowed at school that day and were instructed to go home and to return the next day without their friends and unarmed. Regular classes were cancelled for the next few days, but all students were expected to attend school and take part in small group discussions (led by a skilled teacher or administrator) to understand the thoughts and feelings of all involved. The local police were available if needed, but not deployed on the school grounds. Their accessibility seemed to be enough reassurance, and the expertise of the school personnel was trusted.

The talks went remarkably well and students' eyes were opened to the culture shock that these new students must have felt, along with feelings of resentment, insecurity, and fear of rejection and discrimination. The students all learned that their feelings were unfounded and unnecessary. Quickly, these students gained acceptance into this school and made many close friendships; many excelled academically and some became school leaders.

Certainly progress was made and the equity and safety issues were well addressed within the school, but still these students had to go home to their community, which was/is besieged with drugs and violence. Even with different school opportunities, these bussed students still must have had difficulty excelling to their fullest potential academically when their safety needs were still not fully met outside of their school area.

Then there are the numerous cases and concerns over hidden dangers within our schools that have been written about extensively. Such concerns as subtle assumptions and policies regarding youth, including labeling, testing, and even environmental toxins, are very real safety concerns.

Also, through research on global voices/global visions, conducted over the last several years, a very concerning theme was identified involving a *culture of violence* that seems to infiltrate many countries. These matters, along with a long history of safety concerns impacting youth, including many of the more current horrific events documented by the media, have driven me to get more information and hopefully more answers on the issues at hand.

Thus, the significance of this research is profound. Clearly our youth are the future of our communities and our global society, yet there is considerable dispute on the factors that undermine the safety of youth and feed into this culture of violence. Therefore, research from interdisciplinary fields including psychology, sociology, economics, political science, criminal justice, and even neurocognitive studies and public health perspectives are needed to fully grasp the underlying issues. This was the starting point of the gathering of research to more fully understand the complexities involved.

Thus, the *Developing Safer Climates* project involves archival research, questionnaires, and in-depth interviews. First, a review of available research on current understanding of safety concerns, policies, and interventions will be conducted. Nationally, many interdisciplinary experts included in the references have been researched including the U.S. Department of Education and even the Federal Bureau of Investigation, who also have worked extensively on school safety issues. For example, one very enlightening document regarding school violence was published as a joint endeavor by the U.S. Secret Service and the U.S. Department of Education (2002) titled *The Final Report and Findings of the Safe School Initiative: Implications for the Prevention of School Attacks in the United States*. Unfortunately, this report did not adequately consult with the vast amount of accumulated knowledge from educators, psychologists, sociologists, pediatricians, and other public health professionals with child development expertise.

Also, there is a focus within this work upon students at risk. Understanding the emotional issues related to students at risk for potential behavioral problems impacting safety conditions for all children is needed. Since the psychological processes taking place within aggressive children or the victims of violence are, for the most part, invisible, it is very difficult to identify developing problems. Current research using functional magnetic resonance imaging can tell us a great deal from a medical perspective, but this is not helpful when an incident occurs. We must still rely upon observation of behavior and statements from those involved, which is not adequate but a necessary starting point for fuller understanding.

Internationally, such organizations as the United Nations Educational, Scientific and Cultural Organization and the World Health Organization are tremendous sources of information and are included in this work. Additionally, individuals working closely with youth in other countries will be consulted as well.

Next, information was gathered through a combination of questionnaires and in-depth follow-up interviews (when indicated) with local, national, and international experts on childhood safety issues (including some already mentioned), and parents who may have firsthand experience with safety problems within their schools and communities. The questionnaires were distributed through regular mail, email, and/or on an individual basis to agencies and parents locally, nationally, and internationally. Necessary follow-up interviews were conducted through phone conversations, email, or in person depending upon location/accessibility. Data was gathered, organized, and analyzed using Nvivo software (QSR International, Victoria, Australia).

Utilizing a qualitative inquiry and meta-analytical, research-based approach for the existing data and for gaining insight into the global voices of parents and professionals dealing with safety concerns affords a more complete and insightful understanding. As Taylor and Bogdan (1998) state: "The important reality is what people perceive it to be" (p. 3). Furthermore, Graziano and Raulin (2000) indicate that this type of inquiry (utilizing questionnaires or interview schedules) may be used effectively to obtain information from people in their natural settings.

Of course, more qualitative and quantitative studies will be needed. Both types of research are needed to fully understand our educational issues. Problems are best solved using both quantitative and qualitative studies. One approach without the other will only give us part of the picture. It most definitely is the starting place to hear from those who are on the frontlines of concerns for children's safety.

There are limitations to interviews/questionnaires and potential biases. Thus, every effort has been made to ensure the accuracy of information and to express the needs for clarification, follow-up, and further investigation. The responses have been coded using both a traditional approach to organizing, identifying themes, and analyzing data, as well as the use of NVivo software. Themes identified through qualitative analysis have been further validated by information available through government, educational, and other solidly reviewed sources whenever possible.

Additionally, participants have signed permission forms so that their responses may be included where indicated. Through dialogue, innovative thinking, collaboration, and cooperation, we can provide a platform for solving world safety problems. Thus, the research approach mentioned within this chapter should clearly be seen as a beginning with the need for continual ongoing research as dialogue and feedback will be needed as our communities grow and change.

In the upcoming chapters, we will visit the safety issues identified by parents, educators, first responders, and policymakers and see how these concerning themes are intricately woven into the very fabric of the darker side of our society. Due to the complexity of these entwined safety issues, it is more difficult to address. Such interlaced fibers often are a good trait, but when these influences are distorted or harmful, it is like a cancer that is difficult to remove. Ultimately, it will be the healthier aspects of our society that will help us to eradicate these decaying aspects and reweave a stronger fabric and develop a safer climate for our children and for all our communities.

The following students from Southern New Hampshire University assisted with the research for *Developing Safer schools and Communities for Our Children*: Alexa Grande, Jasmine Hutchins, Meghan Klok, Rebekah Legaspi, Skye Maguire, Alyssa Morin, and Laura Towne.

(Note: the views expressed within this book may not reflect the perspectives of all students.)

NOTE

1. John F. Kennedy – Quotes. Goodreads.com. http://www.goodreads.com/author/quotes/3047.John_F_Kennedy?page=3.

Part II

What Are These Safety Concerns?

From mountain lions and tornadoes, to human predators, bullies, and environmental hazards, the safety issues impacting our youth are dynamic, changing, and very complex. The safety concerns that plague our communities, schools, and children vary somewhat depending upon location of the communities. For example, inner city schools may see more gang involvement, whereas rural schools may see more problems such as mountain lions, yet in many cases the threats are quite similar.

Thus, this section will present the concerns using a different taxonomy by looking at dangers from three perspectives. First we'll look at natural disasters, then manmade potential disasters, and then the most concerning of all, the developing/resulting dangerous subcultures within our communities which appear to result from an interaction of some relatively neutral issues and others that are quite toxic.

Chapter 4

The Parent and School/Agency Perspectives

There are many safety concerns on the minds of parents, educators, and community agency members. The apprehensions were quite similar, although the level of concern seemed to vary within these groups. The top problems on the mind of parents, educators, and agency members varied somewhat depending upon their standpoint. Both groups were mostly externalizing their anxieties (each expressed the safety problems as being outside of their family or agency). In part, this may have been a factor related to which individuals decided to respond to the questionnaire.

These self-selected responders may have been parents with children who have experienced problems within the community and/or the parents who are more aware. For example, parents tended to be more concerned about the potential of instability of others and how this may impact their children. Educators and agency members seemed more concerned with individual (student) problems from a family and sociological perspective, concerns that they must cope with on a daily basis. However, after reviewing all of the concerns from both groups, it is clear that there is considerable overlap with safety problems faced within our communities, and it is important to understand these issues from more than one perspective.

THE PARENT PERSPECTIVE

It is noteworthy that almost every parent answering the questionnaire appeared to be in support of the hard-working professionals in our schools and community organizations. However, there were a number of reported concerns within our schools and communities about facilities being underfunded and understaffed. Parents are concerned that teachers do have not enough time and that there is not enough staff for adequate supervision. (More on these issues in the chapter on solutions.)

1. Technology and Media

Beginning with the viewpoint of parents in this diverse New England city, the number one concern involved the problems associated with technology and media. Parents were most concerned with the high rate of violence and sexuality that children are exposed to through media including gaming, social media sites, television, movies, and so forth. Numerous comments involved the fear that children may "develop an insensitivity to violence," have been or may be a victim of cyberbullying and/or online predators, or might become "addicted" to the use of such technologies and not be unable to "unplug."

This data was somewhat surprising in that parents linked the problems of violence and safety as being related to technology. (In and of itself media is a neutral entity; it is how it is used or misused that presents the very real potential for disaster.) Indeed, violence was a thread within most of the top ranking safety fears of parents.

2. Psychological Pressures on Children

The psychological pressures on children were a very close second to the concerns for technology and media. Many of these pressures could be grouped into peer pressures including pressure to engage in early sexual behavior, illegal use of drugs and/or alcohol, and even pressure to take part in bullying to fit in, to mention just a few. However, just as concerning were the pressures on children to succeed including the specific mention of coaches placing too much emphasis on winning at all costs, pressure to attain high grades to get scholarships to help with financial costs, and so forth.

3. Bullies

Next on the parent list came the concern for bullies within the neighborhoods and the schools. Parents answering the questionnaire were the ones who have had children victimized by bullies or had fears that their child will be bullied. (We do know from research that even those who are witnesses to bullying are negatively impacted.) As might be expected, there was not one parent who responded that their child was a bully! The parents of the children who are the bullies may be unaware of their child's behavior, may not see this behavior as problematic, and/or just chose not to respond.

4. Drugs and Alcohol

Here again, we see parents concerned with what might happen when another individual is under the influence of drugs and alcohol, that these drugs and alcohol are too readily available to children, and that children are being exposed to such activity along with the violence within the community related to drug activity.

5. Predators and Abductions

This also made the top five concerns on the parents' list. Clearly, this threat has become a nightmare scenario for all parents with the numerous events that have been highly televised over the last several years involving child abductions and predators. The fears are not just present for the parents of young children; this is also a very real threat to teenagers being taken into child trafficking rings and prostitution.

These top five safety concerns were followed by thefts, transportation issues (getting to and from school safely), drunk driving and texting while driving, environmental concerns, gangs, home and school invasions, and last on the parent list was a fear that their child would suffer from abuse and suicide.

THE EDUCATOR AND AGENCY PERSPECTIVES

Results from this grouping of community members indicated the following:

1. Suicidal threats and behavior
2. Drug and alcohol issues
3. Abuse, neglect, and domestic violence
4. Gangs and bullying issues
5. Problems of domestic violence, homelessness, and medically related injuries, along with fights and vandalism
6. Runaways, prostitution, sexual exploitation, teen pregnancy, HIV and sexually transmitted infections, and forced marriage

1. Suicidal Threats and Behavior

The educators and agency members listed the low income of many families as problematic, resulting in children without proper clothing, nutrition, or medical insurance. There reportedly is a large refugee population in this diverse city, and services are not always available for these people.

Taking a closer look at the number one concern of educators and agency members, it appears these responders were quite correct to be worried about suicide as a serious safety risk. The Centers for Disease Control and Prevention (CDC) refer to suicide as a serious public health issue and that it impacts not only the individual but also has lasting effects upon parents, other students, and the communities.

Suicide is often referred to as violence turned inward, violence against oneself. All suicides are tragic, since help is available for even the most difficult cases. Youth suicides, because of the age of the victims, is even more heartbreaking, and is unfortunately on the rise. The following statistics from the CDC can put this serious issue into perspective:

- "For youth between the ages of [ten] and [twenty-four], suicide is the third leading cause of death. It results in approximately 4,600 lives lost each year. The top three methods used in suicides of young people include firearm (45 [percent]), suffocation (40 [percent]), and poisoning (8 [percent])" (CDC, 2013).
- A nationwide survey of youth in grades nine to twelve in public and private schools in the United States found that 16 percent of students reported seriously considering suicide, 13 percent reported creating a plan, and 8 percent reporting trying to take their own life in the twelve months preceding the survey.
- Each year, approximately 157,000 youth between the ages of ten and twenty-four receive medical care for self-inflicted injuries at emergency departments across the United States. Suicide affects all youth, but some groups are at higher risk than others.
- Boys are more likely than girls to die from suicide. Of the reported suicides in the ten to twenty-four age group, 81 percent of the deaths were

males and 19 percent were females. Girls, however, are more likely to report attempting suicide than boys.

- Cultural variations in suicide rates also exist, with Native American/Alaskan Native youth having the highest rates of suicide-related fatalities. A nationwide survey of youth in grades nine to twelve in public and private schools in the United States found Hispanic youth were more likely to report attempting suicide than their black and white, non-Hispanic peers (CDC).

2. Drug and Alcohol Issues

The misuse and abuse of illegal substance by youth "can impede the attainment of important developmental milestones, including the development of autonomy, the formation of intimate interpersonal relationships, and general integration into adult society," and, similarly, the use of alcohol and illicit substances by youth often leads to adverse health outcomes.[1]

Unfortunately, despite the known risks to the self, and educational and legal interventions, the use of unlawful drugs remains at a high level with our youth having an increased attraction to marijuana.[2]

3. Abuse, Neglect, and Domestic Violence

Abuse, neglect, and domestic violence issues were indicated often as safety issues for the children:

> According to The Child Abuse Prevention and Treatment Act (CAPTA), (42 U.S.C. §5101), as amended by the CAPTA Reauthorization Act of 2010, the existing definition of child abuse and neglect is defined at a minimum as:
> "Any recent act or failure to act on the part of a parent or caretaker which results in death, serious physical or emotional harm, sexual abuse or exploitation; or an act or failure to act, which presents an imminent risk of serious harm." In 2012 there were approximately 3.4 million referrals alleging maltreatment.[3]

According to the National Coalition Against Domestic Violence, domestic violence "is an epidemic affecting individuals in every community, regardless of age, economic status, race, religion, nationality or educational background." (NCADV, 2014, p.1). Domestic violence is the willful intimidation, physical assault, battery, sexual assault, and/or other abusive behavior perpetrated by an intimate partner against another.[4] (NCADV, 2014, p.1)

But the damage is not felt by just the partners involved but by the children as well, the impacts of which trickle down into our communities and schools.

For example, children who witness violence between their parents or caretakers "have the strongest risk factor of transmitting violent behavior from one generation to the next."[5]

Furthermore,

- Male children are twice as likely to abuse their partners and children in the future, continuing the vicious cycle.
- Thirty to sixty percent of offenders of domestic violence also abuse children in the household.[6]

The risks are so great for not only our youth of today, but for our unborn children as well.

4. Gangs and Bullying

Bullying is a huge concern in the schools and communities in the United States. According to StopBullying.gov, bullying is defined as:

> unwanted, aggressive behavior among school aged children that involves a real or perceived power imbalance. The behavior is repeated, or has the potential to be repeated, over time. Bullying includes actions such as making threats, spreading rumors, attacking someone physically or verbally, and excluding someone from a group on purpose.[7]

School bullying statistics in the United States show that about one in four kids are bullied on a regular basis. Between cyberbullying and bullying at school, the school bullying statistics illustrate a huge problem with bullying in the American school system.[8]

Gangs are another issue and whether we want to believe it or not, street gangs are established throughout the United States. According to the U.S. Department of Justice:

> Large national street gangs pose the greatest threat because they smuggle, produce, transport, and distribute large quantities of illicit drugs throughout the country and are extremely violent. Local street gangs in rural, suburban and urban areas pose a steadily increasing threat, transporting and distributing drugs within specific areas. The local street gangs often imitate the larger, more powerful national gangs in order to gain respect from their rivals.[9]

5. Homelessness and Medically Related Injuries

Homelessness and medically related injuries were ranked next in frequency. The medical injuries are well dealt with in the schools and communities. Teachers have some limited training; school nurses become involved, as do ambulances and other medical personnel when needed.

The educators and agency members also listed the low income of many families as problematic, resulting in children without proper clothing, nutrition, or medical insurance. There reportedly is a large refugee population in this diverse city, and services are not always available for these people. This is an area that needs more assistance.

It's disturbing to hear that children within our communities are at such risk and living at a level that makes survival a real concern. This contributes to a less safe community with increased theft, violence, and escapism behaviors. The basic needs for safety of many children are not being met, and the influencing factors are many and intertwined.

Identifying the themes, untangling the related factors, and understanding the resulting fallout is essential to understanding all the contributing threads and emerging complications.

Problems of domestic violence, along with fights and vandalism, were also listed. Despite an active dedicated police force, the current approaches do not seem to prevent the occurrence of such incidents.

6. Runaways, Prostitution, Sexual Exploitation, Teen Pregnancy, HIV and Sexually Transmitted Infections, and Forced Marriage

Additionally, there were concerns of runaways, prostitution, sexual exploitation, teen pregnancy, HIV and sexually transmitted infections, and the mention of a forced marriage reported by educators and/or agency members.

According to the CDC (2013), new data suggest that there are more than 110 million sexually transmitted infections among men and women across the nation.[10] Many of these occur in the population of the younger generation.

Also according to the CDC, the teen pregnancy and live birth rate has decreased and at a low over the past few years (2012). It does appear, however, that there still may be some higher rates within lower socioeconomic status and minority groups. The reason for the decline and discrepancies is not determined.

Runaways are often considered a part of the homeless population. These individuals may be labeled as unaccompanied youth or minors without parental, foster, or institutional care. The numbers on homeless and runaway children are staggering. According to The National Runaway Switchboard, there are approximately 1.3 million homeless youth living unsupervised on the streets, in abandoned buildings, with friends, or with strangers. Additionally, this population is at a higher risk for physical abuse, sexual exploitation, mental health disabilities, substance abuse, and death.[11]

UNDERLYING THEME OF VIOLENCE

It is interesting to note that most, if not all, of the above-mentioned concerns have an underlying theme of violence related to the safety issues. Thus, one way to better understand this information is to look more closely at this theme of violence (i.e., violence can include gangs, bullies, and so forth).

According to the CDC, violence is defined as "the intentional use of physical force or power, against another person, group, or community with the behavior likely to cause physical or psychological harm."[12]

Distinctions also are made between violence in general and youth violence. However, there are ways that these distinctions may help us to better understand (and thus cope with) these safety violations. Violence can involve all age levels either as perpetrators, victims, or witnesses. However, when an adult is involved with violence in any way, the legal issues and interventions may be quite different. Thus the CDC further delineates youth violence as "harmful behaviors that can start early and continue into young adulthood. The young person can be a victim, an offender, or a witness to violence." Youth violence typically includes persons between the ages of ten and twenty-four years of age, although pathways to youth violence can begin earlier in childhood (CDC, 2013).

The CDC further delineates youth violent behavior as including such acts as "bullying, slapping, or hitting," which may cause more emotional harm than physical harm. Youth violence may also include such behaviors as robbery and assault (even without a weapon) that can lead to serious injury and death (CDC, 2013).

It is important to note here that emotional harm can in some ways have more lasting effects than minor physical harm, because the trauma is not obvious; there are no physical injuries, and thus they often are overlooked or considered less serious, when in fact they can be quite serious indeed and result in depression, anxiety, and posttraumatic stress disorder impacting the victim or observer for many years or even throughout their lifetime. (More about this in the upcoming chapter on the psychological fallout.)

The CDC makes a further distinction between youth violence and school violence. School violence, which is so frequently in the news and on the minds of parents, educators, and community agencies, is seen as a subset of the broader category of youth violence.[13]

It is important to understand the terms that are involved, yet at the same time it is critical to comprehend that these subcategories are arbitrary distinctions. For example, bullying can take place within the community or at school. However, when we say school violence, it may too sharply define boundaries so that one institution does not help to take responsibility for violence that may happen at home (cyberbullying) which is directly related to bullying and cliques at school.

Examples of school violence may involve bullying, fighting, use of weapons, electronic aggression, and even gang violence, according to the CDC definition. To be considered school violence, the behaviors must occur either on school property, coming back and forth from school, or during or en route to or from a school-sponsored event. Of course, this definition makes sense, as long as everyone involved understands that the solution to these problems is not just the responsibility of the schools, just as violence that occurs at other times and on other premises is not just the responsibility of the parents or property owners where the violence occurs.

Sometimes, these territorial distinctions are made to determine legal responsibility. It seems that for legal purposes these precise definitions are often used to get out of responsibility, when in fact it will take a concerted effort for all constituents to solve these problems, and in many ways we all have a responsibility to understand our part.

Schools are meant to be safe settings that allow for an optimal learning environment. Any safety violations do indeed disrupt the climate of the school and impact not only the students, but the teachers, administrators, parents, and community members.

In reality, violence is an interrelated problem and happens in many settings. Likewise, violence at home or on the streets greatly impacts the schools in many ways including academic achievement, climate within the schools, mental health, feelings of safety, and so forth. We all need to take responsibility to intervene and help find solutions.

No one is immune to violence in our society. It is a problem for everyone. According to the CDC's Youth Risk Behavior Surveillance System, in 2011 the percentage of high school students who were threatened or injured with a weapon on school property in the United States was 9.5 percent for boys and 5.2 percent for girls.[14]

To understand just how rampant school violence is in the United States compared to other countries, let's take a look at the timelines of worldwide school and mass shootings from 1996 through October 21, 2013. Nineteen were recorded as occurring in other countries worldwide including four in Germany, two in Canada, two in Finland, and one each in the countries of Scotland, Yemen, Norway, the Netherlands, Sweden, Bosnia-Herzegovina, Brazil, Argentina, Azerbaijan, and France.[15]

For this same time period, there were fifty-five school shootings within the United States alone! The school shooting statistics are very alarming and seem to be occurring more frequently, and this is only one type of violence.

Within one week alone (January 12 to 19, 2014), there were multiple news stories from around the country on this very issue:

- On January 14, 2014, a twelve-year-old middle school boy brought a sawed off shotgun to school and shot two students: one is in critical condition the other now stable. The twelve-year-old is in custody. [16]
- On January 16, 2014, a fifteen-year-old student in Philadelphia, NY, brought a rifle to school. Fortunately, a quick thinking (and heroic) teacher was able to get the weapon. (The school was put in lockdown.) [17]
- On January 17, 2014, near Albany High School in Georgia, a sixteen-year-old student was shot in the arm. Although this did not happen directly on school grounds, it was close by and did happen to a student.

It's disturbing to hear that children within our communities are at such risk and living at a level that makes survival a real concern. This contributes to a less safe community with increased theft, violence, and escapism behaviors.

But with all this stated, we do not want to go too far the other way and err on the neurotic side, actually increasing the fear and anxiety within our schools and communities and not really making our schools any safer. In fact, such approaches may actually make them less safe.

Reading through the CDC control and prevention reports, it is clear that through research and experience the U.S. government and the CDC have prepared for almost any imaginable emergency and that is as it should be: a vital part of coping with these problems, but being prepared has not stopped the problems!

There now is an environment of panic and even distrust on the minds of many parents and even the children. Statistics can be misleading and when it comes right down to it the overall numbers may indicate that the crime rate is down, but let's take a look at the statistics from another perspective. After all, even one act of violence against a child is too much. The violence needs to be stopped.

Clearly, our schools and communities are not as safe as we would like them to be and the issues have changed over the years. Over the next several chapters, we will look at these concerns from a wider perspective to more completely understand the worries of parents, educators, and community members and our changing world.

NOTES

1. Retrieved June 21, 2014, from http://www.nccp.org/publications/pub_1008.html. Primary reference: Towey, Kelly, and Missy Fleming. 2006. *Policy and Resource Guide: Alcohol Use and Adolescents*. Chicago, IL: American College of Preventive Medicine and American Medical Association National Coalition for Adolescent Health.

2. Retrieved June 21, 2014, from http://www.drugabuse.gov/publications/drugfacts/high-school-youth-trends.Retrieved June 16, 2014, from www.cdc.gov/acohol.fact-sheet/underage-drinking.htm.

3. According to Child Maltreatment 2012, http://www.acf.hhs.gov/programs/cb/research-data-technology, and U.S. Department of Health and Human Services, statistics-research/child-maltreatment. Retrieved June 21, 2014, from http://www.acf.hhs.gov/sites/default/files/cb/cm2012.pdf.

4. Retrieved June 21, 2014, from http://www.ncadv.org/files/DomesticViolence FactSheet(National).pdf.

5. Retrieved June 14, 2014, from http://www.ncadv.org/files/DomesticViolence FactSheet(National).pdf.

6. Retrieved June 21, 2014, from http://www.ncadv.org/files/DomesticViolence FactSheet(National).pdf.

7. Retrieved June 21, 2014, from http://www.stopbullying.gov/what-is-bullying/index.html.

8. Retrieved June 21, 2014, from http://www.bullyingstatistics.org/content/school-bullying-statistics.html.

9. Retrieved June 21, 2014, from http://www.justice.gov/criminal/ocgs/gangs/street.html.

10. Retrieved June 16, 2014, from http://www.cdc.gov/std/stats/STI-Estimates-Fact-Sheet-Feb-2013.pdf.

11. Retrieved June 16, 2014, from http://www.ncsl.org/research/human-services/homeless-and-runaway-youth.aspx#_ednref1.

12. CDC. *About School Violence*. Retrieved August 10, 2013, from http://www.cdc.gov/ViolencePrevention/youthviolence/schoolviolence.

13. CDC. *About School Violence*. Retrieved August 10, 2013, from http://www.cdc.gov/ViolencePrevention/youthviolence/schoolviolence.

14. Retrieved 12/7/14 from http://www.cdc.gov/healthyyouth/yrbs/pdf/trends/us_violenceschool_trend_yrbs.pdf

15. Retrieved 12/7/14 from http://www.infoplease.com/ipa/A0777958.html Information Please® Database, © 2012 Pearson Education, Inc Timeline of Worldwide School and Mass Shootings
Read more: Timeline of Worldwide School Shootings | Infoplease.com http://www.infoplease.com/ipa/A0777958.html#ixzz3LF7ugwav

16. Retrieved 1/18/14 from http://www.reuters.com/articles/2014/01/16/us-usa-shottings-newmexic0
By Alex Dobuzinskis and Karen Brooks (1/16/14) Boy, 12, faces battery of charge in New Mexico School Shooting.

17. Retrieved 11/18/14 from http://www.huffingtonpost.com/2014/01/16/teacher-secured-rifle-teen_n_4610113.html

Chapter 5

Manmade Dangers Not Addressed by Parents or Agency Members!

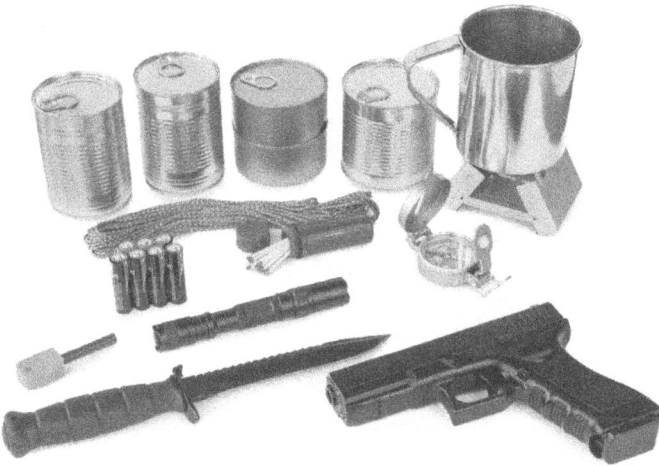

After compiling the concerns of parents and school/agency professionals from participating communities in New Hampshire, it seemed necessary to break these issues down (as well as some additional safety concerns) into two categories: manmade disasters and natural disasters.

In this chapter, we will consider the manmade safety concerns, which are much more predominant, varied, and disturbing to most people and are the predominant worries of both the parents and school and community professionals. So many of the safety concerns that are manmade involve the impacts from advancement in areas such as industry, technology, and even with the tragic choices made by some people. Additionally, statistics are included from a wider look at these concerns from across the United States.

TECHNOLOGY ADVANCES

This sounds like an oxymoron, but even with all of the positive benefits we have from the unprecedented technological advances over the last decade, there are most definitely safety complications. In chapter 4, I mentioned the parents' concerns of safety with this younger generation, but there are even more safety issues not on the radar of parents or responding educators that are potentially problematic.

There have been concerns regarding this plugged-in generation for excess exposure to radiation. Research studies have been conflicting about this issue and the jury is still out. According to the National Cancer Institute at the National Institutes of Health:

> Cell phones emit radiofrequency energy, a form of non-ionizing electromagnetic radiation, which can be absorbed by tissues closest to where the phone is held.
>
> The amount of radiofrequency energy a cell phone user is exposed to depends on the technology of the phone, the distance between the phone's antenna and the user, the extent and type of use, and the user's distance from cell phone towers.
>
> Studies thus far have not shown a consistent link between cell phone use and cancers of the brain, nerves, or other tissues of the head or neck. More research is needed because cell phone technology and how people use cell phones have been changing rapidly. [1]

Since the technological advances are developing at such a rapid pace, research regarding possible safety concerns is lagging well behind. Caution seems to be the best option until more research becomes available, but I do not want any child to suffer the potential devastating consequences as we await more information.

Additionally, there are serious concerns regarding the distractibility issues while driving. Teenagers already have a very high accident rate, in part due to their inexperience, and partly due to their developmental level and not fully comprehending the risks involved. According to the Centers for Disease Control and Prevention, car accidents are the number one cause of death of teens. Approximately 2,800 teens die every year as a result.

Teens are considered high-risk drivers, but they are not the only ones who are driving while distracted. There is a high rate of talking on the phone and even texting or reading texts while driving among U.S. drivers, putting us all at risk, including innocent pedestrians. [2]

Technology has even altered the ways that we make friends and socialization in general. Although concerns with online predators was addressed in Chapter 4, there are indeed real worries affecting some children; even more children are impacted when their physical activity level is decreased. Many children are now less likely to be outside playing in the fresh air and more likely to be playing video games or texting friends, having a very real effect on their physical and mental health.

Our world is definitely changing as the result of technological progress, some ways for the better and some ways adding to the manmade risks to which our children are exposed.

HUMAN TRAFFICKING

Abductions and predators were briefly discussed in chapter 4, but related to these issues and not brought up by the New Hampshire responders is the very real danger of human trafficking involving childhood slavery, prostitution, and drug smuggling. Think this cannot happen in our communities? Think again; it is unfortunately happening in many of our neighborhoods. Human trafficking is yet another manmade danger involving the seizure of mostly children and adolescents into a life of prostitution, drug muling, and slavery. Unfortunately, the rampant illegal use of drugs and alcohol within our culture keeps this danger very much alive because of the greed and lack of humanity of a few sociopathic individuals.

NUCLEAR POWER

Even the unlikely occurrence of a power plant meltdown is unfortunately a possible reality that is one more manmade serious potential disaster that needs more planning. This is not just a science fiction occurrence; it has happened before and with devastating consequences. For example in Chernobyl, Ukraine, in April of 1986, there was a meltdown that affected tens of thousands of people, and the land is still not safe today.

It can happen here, too, as we know from the Three Mile Island Unit 2 reactor partial meltdown that occurred on March 28, 1979, near Middletown, PA. This manmade disaster could have been much worse and ongoing research was conducted monitoring the potential health implications for people possibly exposed to a higher than normal level of radiation.

Agencies involved with research and investigation included the Nuclear Regulatory Commission; the Environmental Protection Agency; the Department of Health, Education, and Welfare (now Health and Human Services); the Department of Energy; the Commonwealth of Pennsylvania; and several independent groups. Reports suggest that the radiation exposure was not excessive for those involved.[3] Nonetheless, our current policy of having an iodine pill ready for every school child is not adequate preparedness or protection in the face of such a crisis!

WARS AND TERRORISM

An example of a potential manmade disaster involves the possibility of an act of terrorism, both foreign and domestic, for these are clearly carried out by man and are destructive. We can include wars in this category as well. The harm goes well beyond the loss of human life and destruction of property, for it unwittingly reinforces a way of dealing with problems through power and violence.

Such acts are based upon misinformation of one another (we are all really more the same in our humanness) and based upon revenge. In fact, according to the writings of Dr. Paul Ekman in his conversation with the Dali Lama, in some parts of the world children are taught resentment and to hold onto anger from actions of others in the past. This tends to motivate students and others to want revenge (2008, p. 194).

We can get stuck in the past by harm that has been caused (in some cases devastating) to thousands of innocent people, such as that which occurred on 9/11 in our own country. But here, too, is an example of the need for a higher order mindset, one that certainly does not forget the heinous crimes that were committed, but that allows for us to make more intelligent choices, to understand the issues involved, thus not allowing for a continued cycle of violence in the future. Revengeful thinking only allows the nemeses to have control by keeping us in a state of being a victim and waiting for revenge. This mentality creates a vicious cycle of violence. The cycle must be broken.

OTHER MANMADE POTENTIAL SAFETY CONCERNS

This is an area I have written about extensively before in *Hidden Dangers: Subtle Signs of Failing Schools* (2008, 2011) and *Hidden Dangers to Kids' Learning: Parent Guide to Cope with Educational Roadblocks* (2010, 2011). However, the issues involved with these manmade concerns need mentioning here again because of the enormous impact they have upon the safety of our children, schools, and communities. Indeed, many of these issues may play a key role in some of the toxic changes we are seeing within our society.

With that said, it seems appropriate to begin this discussion with a look at some of the policies, practices, and even attitudes that have developed in our schools over the years.

POLICIES AND PRACTICES

Dysfunctional policies also create manmade potential disasters. For example, to name just a few:

- When the legal system does not protect those acting to intervene to protect children in danger. Even adults are conflicted as a result of violating individual liability rules, confusing the immediate and appropriate interventions needed to assist a child in danger, as recently occurred when a school bus driver had to sit helplessly by while a child was severely beaten.
- The needs of homeless (often involving children and divorced mothers), displaced refugees including children who cannot return to their countries, and other marginalized populations are creating additional strains and safety problems for our children and communities. Basic needs must be met for food and shelter to cut down on theft and violence.
- Gun accessibility and too easy access to all types of information that we do not need, but we also don't want to live an in overly regulated and censored environment. We still want our rights and freedom, but when should freedom be limited?

Within our schools, some policies also may be counterproductive to establishing a safe environment. For example:

- Zero tolerance is there for the protection of children. It sounds great on paper, but may in fact discourage some children from going to authority figures when they are concerned about a classmate, due to the inflexibility of such rules.
- Safety drills may actually make some children more anxious about the safety of their schools when the practice may be too real with armed police and so forth. Or some students may actually get caught up in the excitement, thus encouraging the very behavior we are trying to prevent!
- Even the labeling/diagnosing of children can single them out and set them up to be targets of bullying and loners within their schools and communities.
- Curriculum choices and teaching approaches also need to be made in terms of safety. For example, I have heard of teachers who use Hollywood movies with all the intensive violence and drama to get students interested in history lessons. Although this may well get students interested, unfortunately they are learning lessons not intended.

And also within our schools, there are problems that policies have not remediated, such as:

- Inequities, including racial, gender, and socioeconomic differences. Our schools are some of the most inequitable in the world despite our laws against such practices. Inequities breed frustration, anger, and at times retaliation.

- Pushing kids too hard is another serious safety concern. On the one hand pushing too hard increases the stress level to overwhelming levels for some kids, resulting in mental health and physical concerns. On the other hand, telling children that they are doing great when they are not only undermines self-esteem as well as the academic success of our future generation.

Such dangerous attitudes include beliefs such as:

- "Kids need to toughen up," suggesting that being bullied or even being a bully is somehow a necessary part of growing up. Clearly, this is an uneducated belief and puts many children at risk throughout their lifetime.
- Pushing kids too hard in any area, but I have particularly observed this with some sports related activities such as cheerleading (flying higher and keeping weight down) and with track. In some schools, children are ex- pected to push themselves until they vomit or they are told they have not tried hard enough. (Not only have I heard this expressed, but all one has to do is observe a track meet where the lined trash barrels are at the finish line waiting!)
- Of course, on the other hand, not getting enough exercise and not testing one's abilities is just as problematic, but there is a healthy balance that we need to help each child find. (It should not be to score another win for the coach.)
- "If it was good enough for me, it's good enough for kids today" is short sighted thinking. (The world and our schools are different places than they were thirty years ago, even ten years ago.)
- "Boys will be boys" perpetuates the gender trap that boys find themselves stuck within where it is less acceptable for boys to express their feelings. In some instances, this may ignite a potential pressure cooker situation.

Most likely, you can think of some attitudes that you have encountered that become common sayings and beliefs within our culture and have devel- oped from a different era. Such outdated ideas and uninformed attitudes can be very harmful indeed.

HAZARDOUS PHYSICAL ENVIRONMENTS

The physical environment can also present serious safety problems for our children, educators, and community members. Older buildings in need of maintenance are often riddled with known hazards such as asbestos, lead paint, and toxic molds. Many of our current school buildings are quite old, and these hazards are present to some extent. Even up-to-date buildings may have issues with radon, which is not necessarily required to be monitored within our homes or schools.

We have been looking at the effects of advancement in areas of technology, manufacturing, and even with the development policies. Although these innovations are in so many ways positive to our society and really overall quite neutral in nature, they do bring with them the potential for misapplication and/or misuse of these developments in ways that can be quite hazardous to our children and communities. However, these manmade "concerns" also bring us a ray of hope in that we have choices we can make to help control these issues. In the next chapter, we will consider the natural disaster safety issues.

NOTES

1. Retrieved June 22, 2014, from http://www.cancer.gov/cancertopics/factsheet/Risk/cell-phones.

2. Retrieved June 22, 2014, from http://www.cdc.gov/media/releases/2013/p0314_driving_mobile_device_use.html.

3. Retrieved March 18, 2014, from http://www.nrc.gov/reading-rm/doc-collections/fact-sheets/3mile-isle.html.

Chapter 6

Natural Disasters

With the ever-present threat of natural disasters including tornadoes, hurricanes, tsunamis, earthquakes, and even volcanoes, it is clear that these are somewhat dependent upon where one lives. Nonetheless, there is no locality that is removed from the potential dangers of the weather.

Yet what is rather perplexing about the information gathered from parents is that these concerns do not seem paramount on their minds as threats to their children. Actually, not one parent mentioned the natural potential dangers as a safety concern. (Although the sample is indeed limited, this begs the question: Do we need to wait until a disaster strikes and the lives of children and others are threatened or lost, before we take reasonable precautions?) An effort to explain the omission of such concerns for potential natural disasters brings up several potential questions:

1. Is there a strong defense of denial operating here, as we seem to be seeing with many people who deny the occurrence of global climate change? (Such denial can be a strong force, even in the face of well-documented research and the actual changes we all have been witnessing over the past few years of the icebergs melting, animal habitats at risk, and increase in and intensification of various forms of weather.)
2. Are there so many other threats to safety that natural disasters need to be put on a back burner, so to speak?
3. Do people think that there is nothing that can be done to control the weather, thus whatever will happen will happen anyway?
4. Do people believe that advances in meteorology and the Federal Emergency Management Agency (FEMA) are protecting them and their children as much as possible?

Whatever the thought process or the situation, there is so much more to consider than just the actual natural disaster itself. Taking a look at the effects of a few natural disasters and the resulting impacts is eye opening. These statistics may be looking globally, but the disasters could occur anywhere.

For example, since the first half of 2013 alone, there have been many documented natural disasters including the 2013 floods in Europe. The financial cost was estimated at more than sixteen billion dollars according to a leading insurance company. Many of the same areas were hit by floods in 2002 as well. (Zürich Insurance Group, 2014)

In 2004, the world was horrified by the tsunamis in the Indian Ocean, and in 2011, a tsunami triggered by an earthquake caused a core meltdown of a nuclear power plant which impacted millions of people, and is still a major concern. (This nuclear meltdown is a result of the interaction between potential manmade disasters and natural disasters.)

Closer to home, in May 2013, one of the deadliest tornadoes in history hit Oklahoma, causing losses of about 3.1 billion dollars, of which only 1.6 billion was covered by insurance.[1]

Depending upon where one lives, even the possibility of a volcano may need to be considered and plans made in the event of hazardous situations. As is the case with so many of these natural disasters, the science of forecasting is improving, but still is based upon statistics and thus some degree of uncertainty. Making forecasts that are in error costs time, money, and numerous resources; not making critical forecasts may cost all of the above as well as the lives of many.

THE IRREPLACEABLE AND LONG-TERM ISSUES

Thus, the time and financial costs are not the most worrisome issue. The most heart-wrenching effects are the loss of life and physical and emotional harm (both in the short-term and long-term). Then we have the irreplaceable loss of personal possessions that further the impact of emotional trauma. Such losses can lead to severe psychological trauma to those directly impacted, but also to first responders, relatives and friends, and even those that have observed the catastrophe.

However, the shadow side of our humanity seems to rise up during times of crisis as well. With some people there ensues a survival process that involves taking whatever they can get at the expense of others; we see such behaviors as looting on the increase during disaster periods. Yet, not all people stoop to such behaviors; for we also may see the most healthy of human behaviors occurring where people may put their own lives at risk to help others, and an outburst of caring ensues with philanthropic actions to assist those in need.

The massive 9.2-magnitude earthquake on the Island of Sumatra, which occurred on December 24, 2004, demonstrates the far-reaching impacts of a natural disaster. The loss of life has been estimated between 300,000 to 350,000 people, leaving in its wake orphans, homelessness, an elevated risk of disease from contaminated water, loss of food, and loss of schools. The list of loss goes on and on with the trauma experienced.

Yet, the impacts do not end there! This earthquake was so strong that it caused a series of deadly tsunamis that devastated Indonesia, India, Madagascar, and Ethiopia. The tsunami was so strong that it actually sped up the rotation of the Earth, and the earthquake so powerful that the Earth actually vibrated by approximately 1 cm. [2]

U.S. NATURAL DISASTERS

Here in our own country, we have seen devastating natural disasters as well. Although this book certainly will not go into every incident because of the numbers of events, it is important to take a closer look at a few. (Just watch the nightly news or the Weather Channel to see how frequently parts of our country are shattered by natural disasters; it is far more common than one might expect.)

In August of 2005, Hurricane Katrina (which grew into a category 5 hurricane) killed an estimated 1,836; millions of others were injured, left homeless, or orphaned, and without many of their community resources including schools, churches, hospitals, and local emergency services. Even such basics as potable drinking water and sanitary conditions were unavailable for many.

The United States found out very quickly how underprepared we were for such a crisis. The political fallout was far reaching with blame being placed on local, state, and federal officials. Bottom line, high-ranking officials were forced to resign, but in reality, it was not just a few people at fault: the emergency management system was not adequate to deal with such emergencies.[3] The effects of Hurricane Katrina are still being felt today, some nine years later.

Then there was Hurricane Sandy (also nicknamed Superstorm Sandy and even Frankenstorm Sandy). This storm developed steadily late into the October 2012 hurricane season. It slammed into the New Jersey shore during a full moon high tide. In Manhattan, ocean water spilled over into the highways, tunnels, and the subway system. "Skyscrapers swayed and creaked in winds that partially toppled a crane [seventy-four] stories above Midtown. A large tanker ship ran aground on the city's Staten Island."[4] Gas stations were closed, airlines cancelled fifteen thousand flights around the world, and nearly 8.5 million people within fifteen states were without electricity.[5] Although we were somewhat more prepared than during Katrina, had Sandy progressed to the strength of Hurricane Katrina, the loss would have been even more catastrophic due to the highly populated area which is not used to getting hurricanes on a regular basis.

In May 2013, Oklahoma was hit by a shattering EF5 tornado with a path as wide as 1.3 miles and 17 miles in length. The tornado warnings were issued by the National Weather Service, but still so many perished. At the Plaza Tower Elementary School, several children and staff members died despite taking available precautions.[6] The problem was that what was available for protection was far from adequate in this tornado-likely area.

Since the 2012 Oklahoma tornado that devastated the town of Moore, children in this community are receiving skating helmets, which may help to some small degree, but are no real answer to the power of a tornado which has the force to catapult a 2×4 through the side of a building.

Not only are the obvious safety issues present during such times of natural disasters, but when children, families, and even whole communities are at risk, people's thoughts and behaviors change into a "survival mode" where maintaining life is more essential than learning to read, write, and think scientifically. When a crisis mode is prolonged, which can happen when protection and necessary resources are not available in a timely manner, when the psychological effects of trauma are not dealt with, or when there is fear of continued hazards without effective and adequate policies and protection in place, the greatest danger may be to our country's future.

If the younger generation grows up in fear and operating in crisis mode, thus not able to focus on the higher order needs including learning, they will be ill prepared to take over the leadership roles within government, schools, or even within their own families. (The reader may want to refer to Maslow's Hierarchy of Needs for a more in-depth understanding of our basic needs.) We will focus more in depth on these issues within the upcoming chapter on mental health concerns and the silent casualties.

So, even with natural disasters there is much more we can do. Yes, the field of meteorology has made great advances; we do have the National Oceanic and Atmospheric Administration (NOAA), which is a U.S. federal government agency.

"NOAA's roots date back to 1807, when the Nation's first scientific agency, the Survey of the Coast, was established. Since then, NOAA has evolved to meet the needs of a changing country. NOAA maintains a presence in every state and has emerged as an international leader on scientific and environmental matters."[7] Some of the tasks charged to NOAA include daily weather forecasts, climate monitoring, and severe storm warnings. "NOAA's dedicated scientists use cutting-edge research and high-tech instrumentation to provide citizens, planners, emergency managers and other decision makers with reliable information they need when they need it."[8] NOAA also is involved with issuing severe weather alerts including for tornadoes, severe storms, and even tsunamis.

NOAA is an excellent organization, but it still cannot totally predict the weather with the complicating climate changes occurring, and it is only one piece in the puzzle of making sure we are as safe from natural disasters as possible.

We also have FEMA, which is another federal government organization that was signed in with an executive order by President Jimmy Carter on April 1, 1979.

FEMA's mission is to support our citizens and first responders to ensure that as a nation we work together to build, sustain, and improve our capability to prepare for, protect against, respond to, recover from, and mitigate all hazards. For thirty-five years, FEMA's mission remains: to lead America to prepare for, prevent, respond to and recover from disasters with a vision of "A Nation Prepared."[9]

Currently, there are more than fourteen thousand FEMA employees across the United States who coordinate "the federal government's role in preparing for, preventing, mitigating the effects of, responding to, and recovering from all domestic disasters, whether natural or man-made, including acts of terror."[10] For a detailed history of FEMA, one may want to access the FEMA.gov official website.

There have been many changes to the agency as the nation experienced different forms of disaster over the years. For example, the the Department of Homeland Security was established and charged with a vital mission... "to secure the nation from the many threats we face." This requires the dedication of more than 240,000 employees in jobs that range from aviation and border security to emergency response, from cybersecurity analyst to chemical facility inspector. Our duties are wide-ranging, but our goal is clear—keeping America safe." (DHS, Updated 2/27/2014, para. 1)[11] Likewise, policies have been established after Hurricane Katrina and Superstorm Sandy. Wild fires that may occur especially during times of drought would also be covered under FEMA.

FEMA has preparedness booklets for what to do in case of such natural disasters as earthquakes and tornadoes, but the real problem is that there is a huge gap between being ready on paper and being ready for the reality of a disaster. It's one thing to have policies and procedures in print, but when an emergency strikes there is little time to refer to such a reference.

Additionally, many schools and places that children and community members frequent do not have adequate funding to provide the safest environment. For example, because of the EF5 tornado in Moore, OK, in May 2013, several school members died, including children at the Plaza Towers Elementary School. Had these people had a safe room to gather in this tornado-ridden part of our country, the outcome may have been better.

Safe rooms are places in a building (home, school, office, or community facility) where people should go when a disaster is pending. As defined by FEMA (2008):

> A safe room is a hardened structure specifically designed to meet the Federal Emergency Management Agency (FEMA) criteria and provide "near-absolute protection" in extreme weather events, including tornados and hurricanes. Near-absolute protection means that, based on our current knowledge of tornados and hurricanes, the occupants of a safe room built in accordance with FEMA guidance will have a very high probability of being protected from injury or death.[12]

COORDINATED EFFORTS

These arms of the federal government (FEMA, NOAA, Homeland Security) must work closely with the state and local communities where disasters have occurred. At times, it may seem as if there is too much red tape to work through, when service and supplies are in urgent need. Each of the fifty states has an emergency management system. Likewise, each city and town has emergency preparedness programs, and hospitals, schools, etc., each have their own established policies in case of a potential crisis. For example, schools in the participating communities in New Hampshire have several well-prepared safety documents that attempt to address almost any possible danger. One such example can be found at http://bosc.mansd.org/policies/policies-safety.

INNER CITY VERSUS RURAL SAFETY CONCERNS

Here, too, we should talk about the differences in potential natural safety problems between rural and inner city communities. For example, it would be much more likely for a dangerous wild animal to come in contact with schools and communities in more rural areas and thus specific policies and community members would be more familiar with dealing with these occurrences.

However, on occasion this can happen in cities as well, particularly as our communities expand further and further out or as climate changes impact the habitat of wildlife. The paths of citizens and animals are more likely to conflict. Take for example the mountain lion that was spotted near a middle school in the spring of 2012 in Southern New Hampshire (Armstrong, 2012). (Southern New Hampshire is fairly developed, with a very diverse population; mountain lions are not a regular occurrence!)

Clearly, one can see from these examples that the natural disasters are not usually within the direct control of parents, teachers, and first responders. However, through research, awareness, preparedness, and prompt action when a natural threat arises, we can keep our children and communities as safe as humanly possible.

In the next section, we will be taking a step to developing safer climates by more fully understanding the dynamics of these safety issues. We will learn that certain factors appear to influence the likelihood of continuing on a self-defeating path. Understanding these factors may help us make more positive choices toward developing a "healthier" community.

NOTES

1. Retrieved August 17, 2013, from http://www.weather.com/news/europe-floods-2013s-costliest-natural-disaster-20130709.

2. Retrieved July 18, 2013, from http://www.universetoday.com/39319/effects-of-tsunamis/#ixzz2ZQAj32Dj.

3. Retrieved March 8, 2014, from http://www.livescience.com/22522-hurricane-katrina-facts.html.

4. Retrieved March 8, 2014, from http://www.livescience.com/24380-hurrican-sandy-status-data.html (paragraph 5).

5. Retrieved March 8, 2014, from http://www.livescience.com/24380-hurrican-sandy-status-data.html.

6. Retrieved March 8, 2014, from http://www.cnn.com/interactive/2013/05/us/moore-oklahoma-tornado/.

7. Retrieved June 3, 2014, from http://www.noaa.gov/about-noaa.html.

8. Retrieved June 3, 2014, from http://www.noaa.gov/about-noaa.html.

9. (FEMA, Updated 8/14/24, para. 1) Retrieved 12/7/14 from https://www.fema.gov/about-agency

10. (FEMA, Updated 8/24/14, para. 1) Retrieved 12/7/14 from https://www.fema.gov/about-agency

11. (FEMA, Updated 8/24/14, para. 1) Retrieved 12/7/14 from https://www.fema.gov/about-agency

12. (Fema, Update 10/15/14, para 1.) Retrieved 12/7/14 from https://www.fema.gov/safe-rooms

Chapter 7

Sick Society Syndrome: The Psychology of the Darker Side of Our Ailing Society

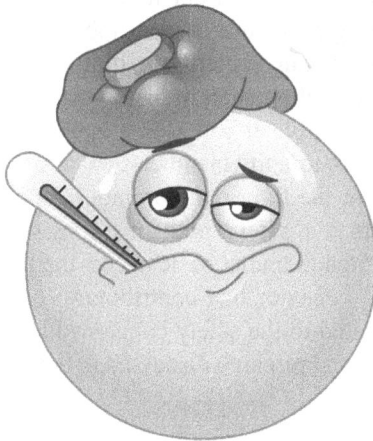

If we wish to help humans to become more fully human, we must realize not only that they try to realize themselves, but that they are also reluctant or afraid or unable to do so. Only by fully appreciating this dialectic between sickness and health can we help to tip the balance in favor of health.
–Abraham Maslow

Much of our society is very healthy, no doubt about that, we are a giving society made up of people that are caring and willing to volunteer their time, expertise, and resources when there is a critical need. When disaster strikes, our communities mobilize to help one another: efforts that go well beyond the national and local organizations that are well established to help during such emergencies. We are talking about the brave individuals that protect our children, even at the cost of their own safety in the face of danger, and the compassionate individuals that give tirelessly of their skills helping people to rebuild their lives. We also are a society that values education and research.

However, we have another side of our society's personality, a darker side that, at times, seems to cast a shadow over the health and well-being of our communities. This murky side is unwholesome and appears to be riddled with themes that are harmful and put our children at risk; thus, I call it the sick society syndrome.

A syndrome is a set of symptoms (or indicators) that characterize a disease or condition, according to the *Webster's New World Dictionary*. The themes identified are indeed the indicators of our concerning safety issues within our society. The symptoms or indicators of the ailing side of our society appear to be made up of at least three components, as we can see from the following figure.

It is this darker side that is so concerning, and each component seems to have many facets that influence the safety of our children and our communities. It is these symptoms that seem to fuel the fallout from a lack of balance in the fast-changing nature of our global world. Although many of the changes occurring in our society are quite positive and allow us to progress at a pace never before seen in history, the impacts of such change are often riddled with negative effects which may decrease the safety of our children; indeed, of all community members.

As you can see from the figure, the ominous aspects of our society that appear to contribute to our safety problems consist of negative attributes (including, but not limited to unmet basic needs, inequities, and disturbances in thought, affect, and behavior that contribute to our ailing culture) all of which appear to be related to the safety concerns identified by parents, educators, first responders, and research discussed in the previous chapters.

Sick Society Syndrome :

The Darker Side of our Society

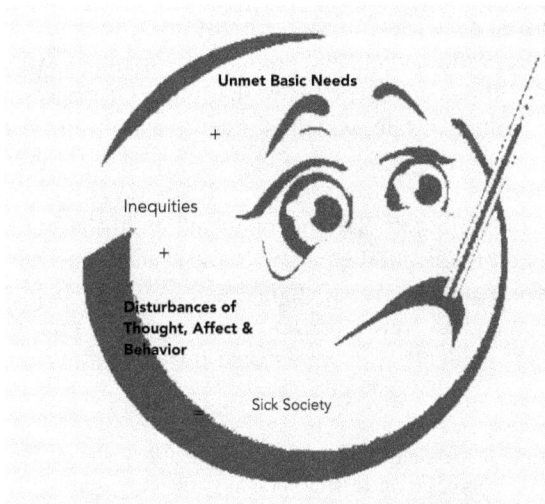

Unmet Basic Needs

+

Inequities

+

Disturbances of
Thought, Affect &
Behavior

Sick Society

Thus, our Sick Society Syndrome = Unmet Basic Needs + Inequities + Disturbances in

Thought, Emotion, and Behavior

There are indeed some very concerning themes that become apparent when analyzing the responses to the safety questionnaires, reviewing current and previous disasters, as well as researching the statistics. The conclusion is that this darker side causing the sick society syndrome can be better understood in terms of unmet basic needs and inequities, along with changes in the thoughts, feelings, and actions of many within our communities; indeed, a cultural shift is occurring.

UNMET BASIC NEEDS FOR SOME

This first major indicator of an ailing society contains several concerning realities. Many of our young children and community members have basic needs that are not met, including lack of shelter, adequate nourishment, and a sense of belonging.

1. **Lack of safe shelter and basic nourishment:** As we know from the classic work of Abraham Maslow, our basic needs must be met in order to attain higher levels of functioning. The most basic needs include the need for air, water, nourishment, and shelter (In Schultz & Schultz, 2013). When people are lacking in basic needs, they may resort to more primitive actions to ensure their existence. It is difficult for some to imagine that there are many people (including high rates

of children) that live on the streets or in inadequate housing, and have little nourishment.

2. **Feeling unsafe within homes, community, and schools:** Indeed, it appears from the parents and community members who responded to the Safer Climates Questionnaire that many of our community members are feeling unsafe, which is a very basic need for our society to flourish.

According to a Public Safety Survey conducted in 2011 from Federal Signal Corp (a public communication equipment and systems manufacturer): "Half of Americans feel they are less safe today than they were before the Sept. 11, 2001, terrorist attacks in New York and Washington."[1] Furthermore a study of 243 fifth-grade students who were asked if they had felt unsafe at school showed that:

> Fifty-seven (23.8 [percent]) participants indicated they sometimes or always felt unsafe at school, citing teasing, bullying, or other threats that typically occurred when adults were not present. Of these, nearly a third reported being stressed and almost half felt at slight or great risk because of feeling unsafe. When children feel unsafe in school, there are implications for schools, neighborhoods, and larger communities.[2]

Considering the theme of isolation, or a lack of a sense of belonging suffered by many of our community members, one wonders if we have taken our value of individualism too far. Most Americans are not selfish people, but is it possible that we have forgotten the importance of each individual including the homeless, the refugees, the mentally ill, and other marginalized individuals? It does seem that many people are not fully accepted in our society. Likewise, many children are ostracized within their schools, as witnessed through increased acts of bullying, acting out behavior, and children on medications for anxiety, depression, and attention problems.

Such an unstable community where individualism is respected only for some and there is a lacking sense of community for all sets the stage for dangerous situations to develop including increased mental illness, anxiety disorders, depression, suicidal ideology, and acting out behavior sometimes in a violent manner to gain recognition, to name just a few. Bullying, cliques, and gangs are on the rise, further complicating the development of healthy communities.

Also, analyzing individualism from a different lens, one wonders if we may have taken this value too far as well, where the need to get ahead becomes more important than the needs of the community as a whole. This is competition run amuck and leads us directly into the next symptom.

INEQUITY

Inequity is seen within our country in so many ways. The reader may be surprised to realize that even though there are laws protecting the rights of the individual and the right for every child to receive an equitable education, the schools in the United States are some of the most inequitable in the world (Darling-Hammond, 2007).

Inequity breeds anger and resentment, and results in generations of young people not prepared to meet the demands of society, creating a self-defeating cycle of failure, which may include less than desirable behaviors of these individuals and perpetuates the problems for future generations. Unmet needs for shelter, nourishment, medical care, and loving homes also place so many youth at risk.

DISTURBING THEMES IN THINKING, FEELING, AND BEHAVIOR

Thinking/Cognitions

Let's begin with the thinking changes that are worth noting from both the responders as well as archival research.

Obliviousness

Is our ailing society gravitating more toward becoming a culture of denial, suppression, and/or lack of awareness? It was perplexing to find that so many parents and educators were either unaware or unmindful of so many of the manmade safety issues and the potential for natural disasters within their own community. Possibly, it was these unmentioned issues that they may believe are totally out of their control, or that our national-, state-, and/or community-level policies have taken care of these potential dangers.

However, as we have seen, in many cases nothing could be further from the truth. Take for example the denial by many of the drug and alcohol problem we have in our schools and in some cases our own children, or the suicidal behavior among our youth. It may be very hard for parents to see that their own child may fall victim to these problems, and teenagers may not feel comfortable confiding in their parents, trying not to worry them.

Another area that appears many are oblivious to is the lack of policies dealing with monitoring radon levels in our schools and our homes. The usage of many toxic substances including cleaners and pesticides, and even the mold in our older schools that tends to go unmonitored impact the health of our children and educators. Asthma rates have skyrocketed, and this may well be a contributing factor (Gunzelmann, 2008, 2012). Even the lack of response to the global warming crisis is evidence of rampant denial within our society.

Distortion and/or Imbalance of Principles

Another aspect of the darker side to our society's personality is the dangers of those with a quest for power. We are seeing examples of this on a daily basis where our senators and representatives are blocking changes the people need for politic reasons. Driven by grandstanding, greed, and biased information is creating an imbalance and distortion of the real issues, of our needs and principles.

Decaying Mores: Beliefs

Certainly this is not a problem with many within our communities, but there does appear to be a developing theme toward a decay of our higher morals and ethical responsibility. We can see this concept through those that are more motivated through greed, and power than through a caring for humanity. A prime example of this involve putting cost ahead of the needs of our children...our future as occurs frequently with the building of schools on hazard brownfields and with the ignoring of the global warming crisis.

Feelings

Negative Mindset

This is the most concerning facet of all. Such an attitude definitely has an influence on our society, with many unhealthy outcomes. Even worrying too much about the safety problems plays into this negativity. We do indeed need to understand the problems, do what we can to prevent or be prepared, and then get on with our lives, and certainly should not burden children with catastrophic thinking. Children learn from what we preach and practice; certainly we do not want to be bringing up a mentally handicapped generation of anxiety-ridden youth.

A negative mindset is a pessimistic outlook. Pessimism has been widely studied by many psychologists over the years. Our perceptions appear to be shifting toward a more pessimistic society. This we need to change.

On the other hand, we do not want to adopt a Pollyanna-type mindset where we naively believe that everyone will be nice and do the right thing if we do. Clearly, what we need in our society is a balanced approach to our thinking.

Apathy

Apathy is not characteristic of most of the citizens of the United States, but I wonder if we are not seeing some symptoms of apathy in our failure to address our current societal troubles of increase in violence, drug and alcohol abuse, and the other ills mentioned within the previous chapters.

Unresponsiveness

Looking the other way and unresponsiveness to the needs of others within our society is more prevalent than any of us would like to admit. This may be a leading cause of the continuation of the inequities within our society.

Social psychologists have studied this issue of unresponsiveness countless times over the last fifty years since the horrific murder of Kitty Genovese in 1964. It is sometimes called the bystander phenomenon and seemed to be the beginning of a sociological drift within our culture that was and still is very disturbing.

Numerous people heard and saw this twenty-nine-year-old woman scream out in distress but failed to act on her behalf. There were reportedly thirty-eight witnesses to the attack, but not one called the police during the approximately thirty-minute attack.[3] One bystander was quoted as saying: "I didn't want to get involved." While another said, "I was tired. I went back to bed."[4]

We live in a hectic, busy world. Our kids are overscheduled, family responsibilities are growing with the increased need for caring for elderly parents, and so many are still out of work as a result of the global economic crisis approximately five years ago. Getting involved takes time and commitment to a cause when so many are already overstretched. Believing that it is someone else's problem or that others will intervene may happen all too often. Such feelings of apathy and helplessness lead to depression and unhealthy behaviors.

Greedy Behavior

One may also argue that we have experienced a cultural shift toward becoming a greedy society. I put this topic under the category of obliviousness, unaware, unresponding, or dare I even say uncaring of the plight of others. You have probably heard the cliché: "It's nothing personal, it's just business." Well, it is personal when out of greed and a lack of ethics we are putting so many in danger.

Making money is not bad; indeed, money is a very necessary requirement to live in a safe and healthy environment. Money itself (like so many of the themes) is a neutral entity. It is how it is managed that appears to be at the source of the problems.

When greed is underlying the management of the monies, a host of un-principled behaviors seem to take hold, creating a culture of greed including media violence to sell movies and gaming industries, drug trafficking, prosti-tution, the get-rich-quick schemes of unethical connivers based upon the fear of parents/teachers, and even the advertising industry that plays up parents' fears to buy unresearched products to protect their child.

Yet another horrific example is the building of schools without adequate shelters from natural disasters such as tornadoes. In Moore, OK, in 2013 a tornado killed twenty-four people including nine children. The elementary school was devastated and had been built without adequate shelter right in the heart of "Tornado Alley" in the United States. Yes, building shelters is expensive, but money should never be more important than the safety of our children and communities. The culture of greed is often fueled by a disregard of ethical behavior, a quest for power, and turning one's back on the needs and fears of others.

RECKLESS BEHAVIOR: CULTURE OF IMMEDIACY

Risk Takers: Have We Taken This Too Far?

We see constant unfortunate cases. Such examples involve many of our youth driving too fast or behaving in a promiscuous manner. Even those individuals not caring to recycle or conserve resources are living as if tomor-row will never come. They seem to live for the thrill of the moment rather than behaving in a responsible fashion, taking in account the needs of others and the future of our planet.

Distorted Convoluted Recreational Activities: Culture of Violence

- Violence as recreation in video games
- Violence linked with relaxation
- Fascination with violence on television and in the news

It should be easy for the reader to see the interrelatedness and overlapping of these darker facets of our society. All lead to a more stressful environ-ment, a pressure cooker full of behaviors that increase safety for our children and communities. The good news is that there are options to make our soci-ety healthier and our communities safer for our children. We will break down these facets in more detail in the upcoming chapters, gaining depth in our understanding of the complexity of the problems by looking at specific fall-out issues and cases reported within our communities in an attempt to fully grasp the problem. Just attempting a Band-Aid approach or willy-nilly reacting out of fear when problems arise will not result in a satisfactory solution to developing safer communities and schools for our children.

These societal shifts are at the top of the list for many parents and educators concerned with protecting their children. All facets/influences together seem to lead to a sick society syndrome, and ultimately toward a more violent culture.

NOTES

1. Retrieved June 26, 2014, from http://americancityandcounty.com/public-safety.
2. Jacobson, Riesch, Kedrowski, Temkin, and C. Kluba (2014). Isolation/Lack of Sense of Belonging Community.
3. Rosenthal, *Times*, or M. Gansberg (1964).
4. Retrieved June 27, 2014, from http://learning.blogs.nytimes.com/2012/03/13/march-13-1964-new-york-woman-killed-while-witnesses-do-nothing/?_php=true&_type=blogs&_r=0.

Part III

Understanding the Problems
Underneath the Problems

It is not enough to just identify the problems. Without an in-depth analysis of the issues at hand, little will be accomplished toward real change. In part III, we delve into the nitty gritty of troubles.

It became clear in chapter 7 on the sick society syndrome that the concerns are extremely complex and interrelated. In the next chapters, we deal with the fallout to our communities in general and consequences to individuals as a result of the changes occuring in our ailing society.

Chapter 8

The Fallout in the Community

The fallout from the themes and issues discussed in the previous chapters result in a tremendous amount of impact for our communities, impacting the safety of our children and ultimately for all individuals. This chapter will explain the consequences within our communities and schools that affect our children and us all. It is not just a few individuals that are impacted by these issues, we all are to some degree.

The residual fallout has a domino effect that exacerbates and perpetuates a drift toward the darker side of our culture: these matters present very concerning penalties indeed. For the sake of organization, I have broken the issues down into related themes, but in reality one issue may result from the influences for several of the themes.

FALLOUT CONCERNS AND CHANGES FACED BY THE COMMUNITY

There have been many changes within our society due to a multiplicity of factors involving elements from an ailing society including the unmet basic needs of many within our country, inherent inequities, and disturbances in thought, emotion, and behavior as well.

Toward a Culture of Violence

The first is a drift toward a culture of violence that is the most alarming of fallout consequences. It is interesting to note that most, if not all, of the previously mentioned concerns from parents, educators, and the available research all have an underlying theme of violence related to the safety issues. We looked in depth at different types of violence and thus, one way to better understand the previous information is to look more closely at this theme of violence.

Violence can involve acts of violence at school or within the community. Youth violence refers to harmful behaviors that may start early and continue into young adulthood. It includes bullying, slapping, punching, weapon use, rape, theft/larceny, vandalism and gangs, and other forms present in our society.[1]

Youth violence results in considerable physical, emotional, social, and economic consequences. Although rates of youth homicide have declined substantially since the mid-1990s, much work remains in reducing this public health burden. Violence is also a major cause of nonfatal injuries among youth. In 2011, more than seven hundred thousand young people aged ten to twenty-four years were treated in emergency departments for nonfatal injuries sustained from assaults. No state is immune to the devastating impact of youth violence.[2]

Although U.S. schools remain relatively safe, any amount of violence is unacceptable. As stated by one community[3]: "Any instance of crime or violence at school not only affects the individuals involved, but also may disrupt the educational process and affect bystanders, the school itself, and the surrounding community."[4]

However, the report indicates that the number of incidents has been rising, after almost twenty years of decline.[5]

And there does seem to be an increase in reports of bullying. It is estimated that approximately fifty-five million students are enrolled in prekindergarten through twelfth grade in the United States, while another fifteen million students attend colleges and universities across the United States. Acts of violence can disrupt the learning process and have serious negative effects on students, the school itself, and the broader community, and may result in law cases and futures disrupted and/or destroyed for many.[6]

The most recent available information is from the annual report, *Indicators of School Crime and Statistics, 2013*, which is a joint project conducted by the Bureau of Justice Statistics and the National Center for Education Statistics. This report specifies the current detailed statistical data on law-breaking offenses in U.S. schools.[7]

During the year 2012, this report indicated that of the greatest concern, there has been an increase in offenses in this newest report, after rates had been declining for almost two decades. Approximately 1.4 million nonfatal victimizations at school includes 615,600 thefts and 749,200 violent offenses for children between the ages of twelve and eighteen years. The rate has increased both on school property from thirty-five offenses out of one thousand students in 2010 to fifty-two offenses out of every one thousand students in 2014. The rate jumped from twenty-seven per one thousand to thirty-eight offenses per one thousand away from school during this same time period.

Regarding violent deaths, although rates of youth homicide have declined substantially since the mid-1990s, much work remains in reducing this public health burden. Homicide remains a leading cause of death among youth aged ten to twenty-four years in the United States.[8] Additionally, significantly higher rates of males are involved in violent offenses.[9] Although studies clearly indicate that violence can vary by ethnicity, we must be careful not to target specific groups of people since violence is caused by other factors within our ailing society, not by differences in gender, ethnicity, and so forth. What is important is to understand the other factors that feed youth violence and to provide appropriate interventions to prevent the total circumstances leading up to violent outbreaks.

Another form of violence, suicide, or violence turned inwards, unfortunately has gradually increased among both sexes for people ten years and older from 2000 to 2009, according to the Centers for Disease Control and Prevention. However, I include suicide within this chapter, but will discuss it more in depth in chapter 9 on the individual.[10] Suicide is an act of violence toward the self which impacts the entire community, not just the individual.

Bullying also is considered an act of violence in that it hurts others and impacts the entire environment, both the school and community. Some environments tend to ignore and not respond to such acts, to disturbingly view bullying as a rite of passage. When bullying is not seen for what it is, an abusive form of violence, the entire community is negatively impacted. By definition, the injury from bullying can involve direct physical offenses, such as hitting, stabbing, choking, burning, and other forms of physical harm, or indirect ways, such as rejecting, isolating humiliating, blackmailing, daring, and cyberbullying where there are no boundaries. (Likewise, bullying will be discussed in more detail within the next chapter where we look both at the bully and the victim.)

Toward a Desensitized Population

Are we becoming a more desensitized population as a result of the ailing parts of our society? The answer is yes, and this presents some very concerning problems.

The fallout from technological advances and mass media included the exploding market for video gaming, movies, and the daily news. There is much concern that we are becoming a desensitized population. Certainly not everyone is insensitive to the feelings of others, but unfortunately many have become numbed to the pain and suffering of others. The causes of this phenomenon are still being researched, but there is evidence to suggest that the vividness of our current technologies including television, computers, cell phones, and the gaming industry contribute to this problem.

Obviously, these advances make viewing easier and more enjoyable, but herein lies the danger. The first is that we see so much violence in our communities, on the news, and through movies, television, and gaming that we may come to expect that violence is the norm. Thus, if we expect violence, then we may indeed bring it on by default.

Some of the foremost research in the U.S. on media violence and the effects of individuals comes for the work of Brad Bushman, D. Gentile and C. Anderson and commands an overview here. For example, when we become desensitized to violence, we become less empathic and less apt to engage in helping others. According to Bushman, these effects occur for males and females, young and old throughout the world (Bushman & Anderson, 2009). Indeed, the impact is not just upon a few individuals, but impacts us all.

We have reviewed the horrific case of Kitty Genovese in 1964 which was studied by social psychologists as a bystander phenomenon where others thought that someone else would respond. The complexities of such a bystander occurrence are really much more complicated than this and may well involve desensitization to others.

Clearly our world has changed quite dramatically, particularly since September 11, 2001. We are subjected to the possibility of more violence and exposed to more violence on a constant basis through mass media modalities. Furthermore, the intensely vivid exposure presented through gaming tends to make even imaginary violence quite real.

Even as far back as 1963 from the classic research by Bandura, Ross, and Ross, there was "strong evidence that exposure to filmed aggression heightens aggressive reactions in children" (p. 9). The researchers go on to state that "Subjects who viewed the aggressive human and cartoon models on film exhibited nearly twice as much aggression than did subjects in the control group who were not exposed to the aggressive film content" (p. 9).

What concerns me the most about this very early research is that we still are not listening! After more than fifty years of continuing research, we still do not want to believe that exposure to violence has a serious side effect for our communities.

More current research from Gentile and Anderson (2003) suggests that violent video games are the newest media hazard. The validity and generalization of these studies have been widely recognized and indicate that playing violent video games increases aggressive thoughts and emotions, and increases aggressive behaviors. The realistic video games increase physiological arousal and because of the interactive nature what children learn is quickly and deeply absorbed. Although there can be conflicting research results, are you willing to risk it?

A quote from Dr. Gentile sums this problem up well and leads us into the next very concerning fallout feature:

> It looks like a pretty clear link. Kids who play more violent video games—it changes their attitudes and their beliefs about aggression. It does desensitize them. It certainly hypes up aggressive feelings in the short-term. In the long-term it probably links aggression with fun, which is a really weird idea. Or aggression with relaxation, another weird idea.

A Disturbing View of Fun and Relaxation

This combination of aggression and relaxation is very disturbing. Indeed, it is as concerning as acts of rape are a strange combination of aggression and sexual behavior, and we have been seeing an increase in violent acts for the purpose of seeing how it might feel, or for the "thrill of it." It does not get more concerning than this.

Toward an Even More Stressed Society

There is no doubt the living in the twenty-first century brings more stress than was felt a half-century ago. Yes, the world has changed, the pace of living is much quicker, and we now need to deal with terrorist threats and to lock our doors at night. Family problems are the norm rather than the exception in many U.S. households partly due to the economic problems, unemployment, and the need for two parents to be employed and away from the home for many hours each day.

Once home, they are confronted by the needs of overly scheduled children and their ensuing problems. The baby boomer generation is aging thus there are many families trying to cope with the needs of their elderly parents with little or no assistance, the costs of which can be astronomical.

Bottom line, even many relatively strong, healthy families are stressed, but add in the dynamics of a struggling or disturbed family and the stress levels soar, impacting all our communities. Unfortunately many families in the United States are experiencing challenging times as a result of mental illness, substance abuse, or physical illnesses. Additionally, many families lack the support of friends or extended family to help in times of crisis often due to the need to relocate for work or estranged family relations.

Couple these issues with unemployment and attempting to raise a family existing at or below the poverty level, being homeless or living in dangerous neighborhoods, and having inadequate education to obtain employment, and the stress levels become unbearable. It does not happen in our country you say? Guess again.

An estimated 14.5 percent of American households were food insecure at least some time during the year in 2012, meaning they lacked access to enough food for an active, healthy life for all household members.[11]

Furthermore, according to an April 2013 report from the U.S. Department of Education and the National Institute of Literacy, it is estimated that thirty-two million adults in the United States are not able to read. Even graduating from high school does not assure literacy as approximately 19 percent of high school graduates are not able to read. And although the unemployment rate in the United States has been decreasing (as of July 3, 2014, it was at 6.1 percent), that still is a lot of families in need of assistance.[12]

It is very difficult for these families to get ahead when their circumstances keep them living on the edge.

Toward a More Marginalized Society

Are we becoming a more marginalized society? Again, there is evidence to suggest that this may well be the case. It does seem that many are living on the fringes of society, and it is happening for other reasons as well. The refugee population/situation in the United States is another example of this problem. Keep in mind the definition of a refugee is a person in dire need.

A refugee, as defined by Section 101(a) 42 of the Immigration and Nationality Act, based on the United Nations 1951 Convention and 1967 Protocols relating to the Status of Refugees, "is a person who is unable or unwilling to return to the home country because of a 'well-founded fear of persecution' due to race, membership in a particular social group, political opinion, religion, or national origin."[13]

The very highest percentage of these refugees are upstanding individuals who contribute greatly and thankfully to our country. Furthermore, as a people, it has not been within our core values to turn our backs on those in need. "The United States is proud of its history of welcoming immigrants and refugees. The U.S. refugee resettlement program reflects the United States' highest values and aspirations to compassion, generosity and leadership. Since 1975, Americans have welcomed over [three] million refugees from all over the world. Refugees have built new lives, homes and communities in towns and cities in all [fifty] states."[14]

Yet, one educator commented that she believed that many of the refugee families were not welcomed by many within this reporting community. This marginalizes this population when they already are at risk due to language differences, lack of employment, trauma suffered in their country of origin, and then unfortunately being shunned by some community members when arriving in the United States where they believed they would find help. I suspect the need of the refugee population is much greater than indicated.

Economic Struggles and Increased Inequities

There does appear to be a conflict between the darker, greedier side of humanity and our strong ethical nature. Money is not an evil entity; it really is quite neutral, just as technology, media, and other manmade enhancements. It is all in how it is used or not used where the problems develop and may indeed tip the scales toward a culture of greed, making our society less safe and even encouraging a culture of violence.

Analyzing the U.S. Census data on poverty and from research from the National Center on Poverty from the University of Michigan, from the 1950s to 2010, several patterns seem to emerge. For example, according to the University of Michigan Center for Poverty,

> During the 1950s, the poverty rate for all Americans was 22.4 percent, or 39.5 million individuals. These numbers declined steadily throughout the 1960s, reaching a low of 11.1 percent, or 22.9 million individuals, in 1973. Over the next decade, the poverty rate fluctuated between 11.1 and 12.6 percent, but it began to rise steadily again in 1980. By 1983, the number of poor individuals had risen to 35.3 million individuals, or 15.2 percent.[15]

Now clearly, the state of the economy and the number of individuals living in poverty are complex issues. Nonetheless, I cannot help but notice the rate of poverty began to rise at approximately the same time that the United States began its educational decline back in the 1980s. According to data from the University of Michigan National Poverty Center, "In 2010, 15.1 percent of all persons lived in poverty."[16]

In 2010, 16.4 million children, or 22 percent, were poor. The poverty rate for children also varies substantially by race and Hispanic origin.[17] Again, we can see the issues of inequity creeping into our discussion, and the economic crisis of the last several years has only exacerbated the problems.

Money is just one of the issues of inequity encountered by many ethnic groups. The racial issues have been very well documented for white, non-Hispanic, Hispanic, and Black children and their families. For detailed information, the reader may wish to access information from the U.S. Census at https://www.census.gov/prod/2014pubs/p70-137.pdf.

However, it is not just those millions living in poverty in the United States that we need to be concerned about. We have another whole population, that of families living just above the poverty level who may not qualify for assistance. According to Charles Hokayem and Misty L. Heggeness (2014), "in 2012, 14.7 million people in the United States had family incomes between 100 and 125 percent of their poverty threshold. The near-poverty rate for individuals decreased from 6.3 percent in 1966 to 4.7 percent in 2012." Level of education has much to do with the number of families living at this near-poverty rate.

Even the youth that may become homeless when their families fall into difficult financial situations resulting from lack of affordable housing, difficulty obtaining or maintaining a job, or lack of medical insurance or other benefits may later find themselves separated from their families and/or living on the streets alone.[18]

Data suggests that the current recession has yielded an increase in homeless and runaway youth. Between 2005 and 2008, the National Runaway Switchboard saw a 200 percent increase in calls from youth indicating economic reasons for running away from home.[19]

Clearly and inevitably, the safety issues are compounded for all members of our communities when survival, shelter, and nourishment issues are motivation for so many within our communities. The stage has been unintentionally set for the societal problems of theft, violence, prostitution, trafficking, drug and alcohol, and all forms of abuse and neglect to be set in motion. Research from the National Poverty Center suggests that poverty raises the costs of crime by about $170 billion annually (Holzer et al., 2007, p. 19). Furthermore, poverty also impacts the health of children (which impacts learning).

Toward an Imbalance in Our Cultural Values

So how does all this data imply that we may be seeing a drift toward a further imbalance within our society? As in any culture, our values are deeply ingrained, but certain circumstances may push the pendulum well out of center, resulting in extreme situations where it may appear that our beliefs are in conflict.

For example, we are a culture that strongly values our individualism and the freedom and rights we have as individuals. Yet, we should possibly be asking: Has our cultural value for individualism gone out of balance to the extent that we are becoming more self-absorbed and less concerned about our fellow community members? It seems this may be the situation when we have so many inequities in educational opportunity and economic advantages.

Are we becoming a greedier and even less ethical society? Why would a business venture play upon people's fears, making our safety problems even worse? We could ask this of the gaming industry where the research has become quite clear on the changes that video violence has on the players, or with the opportunity to make a buck by suggesting that a mere helmet is adequate protection for our children in schools where storm shelters are the necessity. (No problem with having helmets, too, though.)

Clearly, the improvements in technology and gaming can make our world a safer place when used appropriately. Through such advances, the medical field is able to assist our wounded soldiers from afar; robots can take the place of humans when serious safety risks are present and many more. It is clear that it is through such advances that our world will also become a safer place, but it seems more work is being done with gaming that earns the most money despite the known hazards: violent gaming. Ethically, this seems wrong, irresponsible, and greedy on this aspect of this industry.

Imbalance Within Our Government Ideals

And what about the imbalance created within our government where politics places our country in gridlock? Our government has been developed on solid principles that we all hold dear, but these, too, are being challenged. When politics become more important than the individuals that make up this country, when the inequities that are so rampant are not remedied, when hard-working families and children do not have their basic needs met, when health care is not seen as a right for everyone, then we have a system that is out of balance. It will take us working together, not trying to discredit one another, not trying to build one's political career, or retaliating for previous situations.

It will require a commitment from us all to work with our governing leaders to develop research-based policies to remedy the ills of our society. I can just hear the arguments now from those who believe that those who live in poverty and those who are experiencing inequalities will just abuse the system. Yes there are those who may misuse services, but there is still hope for our society. Most of us are good and ethical people, and many are hurting.

Not providing for the less fortunate is not helping to create a safer world. Indeed, it is contributing to our safety concerns.

In the next chapter, we will see the fallout to individuals and understand the impact on a much more personal level.

NOTES

1. According to the Centers for Disease Control and Prevention.

2. Retrieved July 22, 2014, from http://www.cdc.gov/VIOLENCEPREVENTION/youth-violence/stats_at-a_glance/.

3. Brookmeyer, Fanti, and Henrich, 2006; Goldstein, Young, and Boyd, 2008.

4. In National Center for Education Statistics, *Indicators of School Crime and Safety 2013*, paragraph 1.

5. National Center for Education Statistics, *Indicators of School Crime and Safety 2013*; June 10, 2014 NCJ 2432990.

6. http://www.cdc.gov/ViolencePrevention/youthviolence/schoolviolence/index.html.

7. National Center for Education Statistics, *Indicators of School Crime and Safety 2013*; June 10, 2014 NCJ 2432990.

8. Retrieved July 24, 2014, from http://www.cdc.gov/violenceprevention/childmaltreat-ment/index.html.

9. Retrieved July 24, 2014, from http://www.cdc.gov/violenceprevention/data_stats/in-dex.html.

10. Retrieved July 24, 2014, from http://www.cdc.gov/violenceprevention/suicide/statis-tics/trends01.html.

11. Coleman et al., 2012.

12. U.S. Dept. of Labor, 2014.

13. Retrieved June 15, 2014, from http://www.immigrationpolicy.org/just-facts/refugees-fact-sheet.

14. U.S. Department of State, Refugee Information. Retrieved June 15, 2014.

15. National Poverty Center, Poverty Facts, paragraph 6.

16. Retrieved July 27, 2014, from from http://www.npc.umich.edu/poverty/#2.

17. Retrieved July 27, 2014, from from http://www.npc.umich.edu/poverty/#2.

18. Retrieved June 16, 2014, from http://www.ncsl.org/research/human-services/homeless-and-runaway-youth.aspx#_ednref1.

19. Retrieved June 16, 2014, from http://www.ncsl.org/research/human-services/homeless-and-runaway-youth.aspx#_ednref1.

Chapter 9

Fallout: Mental Health Concerns of Individuals: The Often Invisible Injuries

The psychological harm that comes from toxic conditions may indeed be the most crippling and has self-perpetuating cycles, and results in escalating climates of violence, destruction, and safety concerns. Some of these issues impact each and every one of us to varying degrees: susceptible individuals; the victims of bullying, abuse, and neglect; the witnesses to acts of violence; and those individuals suffering from mental illness.

THE CHANGED BRAINS OF INDIVIDUALS

Whether we want to believe it or not, research has indicated that when exposed to violence, changes within our brains actually occur and again the newer research indicates that these brain changes occur to each and every one of us, not just a few more vulnerable indivduals. Weber (2005) from the University of Michigan was able to determine both a link and the short-term causal relationship between violent video game usage leading to brain activity characteristic of aggression on functional magnetic resonance imaging scans. The long-term outcomes of such exposures are yet to be seen, but may well drift our society more into the darker side.

Additionally, Moore (2011) from the Indiana School of Medicine explains that even after one week of violent video gaming, brain activity is altered showing less activity in frontal regions involved with cognitive function and emotional control, a very concerning finding indeed that impacts each individual subjected to this type of violence.

THE FALLOUT OF THOSE INDIVIDUALS INVOLVED IN BULLYING CASES AND OTHER FORMS OF VIOLENCE

The targets of bullying, those excluded by cliques, and undervalued due to individual differences in abilities, race, creed, gender, or sexuality also are at risk from lacking a place within their school or community. According to the FBI such hate offenses included: "Crimes reported to the FBI involve those motivated by biases based on race, religion, sexual orientation, ethnicity/ national origin, and disability. Forthcoming system changes will also allow the reporting of crimes motivated by biases based on gender and gender identity, as well as crimes committed by and crimes directed against juveniles."[1] The shear number of reported offenses are concerning: "According to statistics released today by the Federal Bureau of Investigation, 5,796 criminal incidents involving 6,718 offenses were reported in 2012" (FBI, 2012).

The Victims of Bullying

Most of the bullying incidents involve verbal or some form of mental bullying, which may involve spreading vicious rumors or using belittling terms often related to a person's race, gender, sexual orientation, or religion. It is important to keep in mind that youth are quite sensitive to many of these issues due to their emerging/developing identity. Adolescents tend to be quite critical of themselves, and their brains are not fully developed making it more difficult for some to cope. Many young people suffer tremendously from bullying to the extent that they experience anxiety, depression, and lowered self-esteem and in extreme cases suicidal thoughts or bullycide.[2]

Cyberbullying is a serious threat that impacts thousands of students. Approximately 80 percent of high school students surveyed admitted to being bullied online through Facebook, Twitter, and other forms of social networking.[3] Even more alarmingly, this source says,

> These growing numbers are being attributed to youth violence including both homicide and suicide. While school shootings across the country are becoming more and more common, most teens that say they have considered becoming violent toward their peers, wish to do so because they want to get back at those who have bullied them online. About 35 percent of teens have been actually threatened online. About half of all teens admit they have said something mean or hurtful to another teen online. Most have done it more than once.[4]

The Actual Perpetrators

Many times, the actual perpetrator is not the typical class bully portrayed in movies during the 1950s. Yes, these "typical bullies" still exist, but the problem has become much more widespread where unbelievably according to one report, one in five students admits to bullying their peers.[5] Many of these bullies have grown up in a culture where such behavior has been allowed, ignored, or in some cases even encouraged. The more often youth are exposed to bullying, as with other forms of violence, they learn such behavior and are more apt to act out in such a manner.

Furthermore, analyses of case studies of perpetrators of violence or behaviors threatening the well-being of children often had histories of being bullied and shunned within their communities. One needs to question if these individuals become so angry, so frustrated, so in need of a place to belong that they act out in desperation.

The Bystanders

- The bystanders also experience fallout. By not intervening, they may feel guilty or helpless, increasing their own level of anxiety. If they do choose to intervene, they may experience physical harm or become the victim of bullying themselves. And last but certainly not least, they are witnessing bullying, a form of violence, that changes the person, desensitizes even the bystanders, and they have viewed and learned bullying behavior.
- Children exposed to inappropriate models also incur damage to their development and to the understanding of how to manage emotions. Unfortunately, they learn inappropriate behavior, reinforcing and perpetuating the cycle of violence.

- Not every child will act out in such a manner, but it has changed each individual, and the more frequent the incidents the more "normal" they seem, which is the very essence of the desensitized crisis.

STRESS TO THE INDIVIDUAL

The increasing stress levels we experience as a result of living in our changing, complex world can be quite real, but I am most concerned with our failure to help protect our youth and help them learn to cope with the growing pressures. The community needs to protect youth from the pressure and from unreasonable expectations, help them develop and set reasonable expectations for themselves and learn how to cope. This is essential for each individual.

One of the fallout issues from the overly scheduled, stressed out youth may be our plugged in, but turned off generation of students. Others may turn to drugs and alcohol to lessen their anxieties, which of course, increases the safety concerns. According to the Centers for Disease Control and Prevention (2014), "alcohol and other drug use among our nation's youth remains a major public health problem. Substance use and abuse can increase the risk for injuries, violence, HIV infection, and other diseases."[6]

According to Towey and Fleming (2006), alcohol for youth under twenty-one years is the most commonly used and abused drug in the United States, and may lead to binge drinking, emergency room visits of approximately 189,000, and has resulted in more than 4,300 young deaths.[7]

Although there appears to be a hopeful, downward trend of the abuse of alcohol, the safety concerns speak volumes from the number of deaths, injuries, addictions, emergency room visits, and exposure to HIV/AIDS and other diseases while under the influence. Illegal drug abuse presents problems for many young people as well.

For example, since the mid- to late 2000s, drug use has been on the increase. In 2013, 7 percent of eighth graders, 18 percent of tenth graders, and 22.7 percent of twelfth graders used marijuana in the past month, up from 5.8 percent, 13.8 percent, and 19.4 percent in 2008, respectively. Daily use has also increased: 6.5 percent of twelfth graders now use marijuana every day, compared to 5 percent in the mid-2000s.[8]

Unfortunately, despite the known risks to the self, and educational and legal interventions, the use of unlawful drugs remains at a high level with our youth, with an increased attractiveness of marijuana.[9]

The use of prescription drugs for nonmedical reasons also is on the increase. In 2013, 15 percent of high school seniors used a prescription drug nonmedically in the past year. The survey shows continued abuse of Adderall, commonly used to treat attention deficit hyperactivity disorder, with 7.4 percent of seniors reporting taking it for nonmedical reasons. [10]

Although there is a decrease in the use of some of the hard core drugs (cocaine, methamphetamines, inhalants, and hallucinogens), there is a slight increase in the use of ecstasy. Heroine appears to be abused at about the same rate over the past year. [11]

Here again, we must understand that even when there is a positive trend in the safer direction, the use/abuse of drugs and alcohol creates serious health and safety concerns for us all, and decreases the child's potential by possibly disrupting the developing brain, depriving the young person of being able to learn optimally in school, and causing the child to become dependent upon substances resulting in a lifelong disability.

The World Health Organization reported that "harmful and hazardous alcohol use are risk factors both for being victimized and perpetuating youth violence" (2006).

Furthermore, youth violence reaches across all sectors of society since alcohol misuse by youth increases risk for becoming a perpetrator and/or a victim through decreased inhibition, increased courage, reduced physical control, increased impulsivity, and risk taking.

Victims of violence may also use drugs and alcohol as a way to self-medicate, further putting them at risk as targets due to dismissed awareness and ability to respond. [12]

Even some societal beliefs may increase the chance for aggression due to beliefs of using alcohol to increase courage or in ritualistic ways to show membership in a youth culture gang. Youth gangs exist throughout the world and are often involved in violent acts. [13]

Qualitative research from the United States found a strong relationship between alcohol, gang culture, and violence. Alcohol is being used before fights to increase confidence and after to show unity and as part of initiation rituals into membership. [14]

Certainly there are gender differences with youth violence and alcohol; males are associated with higher levels, but these are increasing statistics worldwide for females as well. And of course if children are exposed to the toxic effects of prenatal alcohol exposure, it can result in fetal alcohol syndrome which is further associated with behavioral and social problems and delinquency. Certain mental health disorders such as antisocial personality disorder may be associated with bouts of heavier drinking and violent behaviors as well. [15]

Of course, we cannot place all the blame on youth turning to drugs and alcohol upon stress. There are other stimuli at work here, including peer pressure and modeling from advertising, films, television, and other influences, but the stress factor also plays a significant role.

Even teenage pregnancy may be an escape for some teens naively hoping to avoid the pressures of youth by running head first into parenting. Unfortunately, most often these child parents only increase the problems for themselves, babies, families, and communities. The good news is that according to the Centers for Disease Control and Prevention, the teen pregnancy and live birth rate has decreased over the past few years (2012). It does appear however, that there still may be some higher rates within in lower socioeconomic status and minority groups. The reason for the decline and discrepancies are not fully realized.

Of course, teen pregnancies can happen for other reasons as well including the violence of rape. Failure of the community to protect youth from unreasonable pressures, from excessive expectations, and not helping them to develop attainable hopes for themselves increase the problems for us all.

INDIVIDUAL FALLOUT AS A RESULT OF NOT BELONGING

> A deep sense of love and belonging is an irreducible need of all people. We are biologically, cognitively, physically, and spiritually wired to love, to be loved, and to belong. When those needs are not met, we don't function as we were meant to. We break. We fall apart. We numb. We ache. We hurt others. We get sick.
> -Brene Brown (Brainy Quotes)

Feeling alone, dejected, rejected, and/or different is a most uncomfortable sensation and significantly impacts the individual and ultimately the climate of others within the community. We know from the work of Abraham Maslow that feeling a sense of belonging is paramount to learning and to functioning at higher levels. Belonging comes right above the safety needs of the individual with only the most basic needs of air, water, and food at the lowest level (Maslow, 1962).

When the belonging needs are not met, it stands to follow that the needs for safety are going to be sought out. As Maslow stated, "you will either step forward into growth or you will step back into safety" (*Motivation and Personality*, p. 19). Yet our foundation of safety is different now than back in the 1950s and early 1960s when Maslow was writing these words.

Today our basic safety level is oftentimes eroded, making a step backward more of a step toward uncertainty, risk, and anxiety. Furthermore, when the most fundamental level is not well established, for whatever the reason(s), economic hardships, homelessness, or so forth, our safety concerns become even more alarming.

When people are not getting enough to eat or do not have shelter from the harsh realities of our environment, they are in a fight for survival, putting safety aside. Although we may want to believe that this is a minority of people struggling at this level, their numbers are great and the risks are real. Current statistics in the United States suggest that 22 percent of all children under the age of eighteen years are living in poverty. The numbers are much higher for children of color. [16]

Interestingly enough, even the brains of individuals deprived of a sense of belonging experience change. As one can imagine, it is difficult to study the effects of isolation on humans (adults or children) due to the ethical problems that would arise from intentionally isolating human subjects in a laboratory setting. Thus, most of the studies have been conducted on laboratory animals.

However, researchers Cacioppo, Hawkley, Norman, and Berntson (2011) are quick to note that "the effects of perceived isolation in humans share much in common with the effects of experimental manipulations of isolation in nonhuman social species" (p. 17). Thus, we have much to learn from these animal models.

Animal models provide us with evidence that the effects of isolation can be quite devastating, increasing stress level, anxiety, and depression; lowering immunity; and even hindering the overall social development of the organism (Cacioppo et al., 2011; also thebrainmcgill.ca).

In a study conducted by Djordjevic, Djordjevic, and Radojcic (2012), results indicated that the effects of chronic social isolation on rats actually changed brain plasticity. Previous studies showed changes within the limbic brain structures, hippocampus, and prefrontal cortex that resembled brain alterations described in studies of depression (p. 112).

On occasion, we have the unfortunate opportunity to be able to study the effects of isolation on human children who have been abandoned through death of caregivers or other tragic situations, and the impacts are significant. One classic study by Rene Spitz back in the 1940s was conducted on children raised in an orphanage over a period of several years. Although these children were fed, clean, and clothed, they did not receive regular human contact and caring due to the overworked and understaffed facility. The effects on the children's development were shattering and included serious physical, intellectual, and social development problems.

Clearly, there are many factors involved, and each child's case is unique. The child's earlier risk factors, genetics, family life, and so forth all play a part, but suffice it to say that I have not read any studies indicating that feelings of prolonged isolation or not feeling a sense of belonging have been beneficial.

How does all this play out into the specific concerns within our schools and communities? It has been noted time and time again by the parent questionnaires and the responses of professional educators that one of the most pressing problems is one of children trying to fit in, but not knowing how. Many are lacking the necessary social skills due to inexperience during critical childhood periods of learning to interact with others, or through certain disabilities where reading the social cues of others is difficult. Whatever the reason, these children are not receiving what they need to help them fit in.

Marginalized Refugees

When refugees first come to our country, they usually have experienced serious trauma and are not safe in the country of origin. Posttraumatic stress disorder is common among our refugee population. Unfortunately, they may even be further traumatized by a lack of acceptance and understanding within our communities.

It is very difficult for some Americans to understand the horrors that many refugees have experienced, and we have little in place to assist the needs of this population within our midst. Of course they need food, shelter, and education. But equally important are their needs to belong and contribute in a meaningful way to their new home.

Gangs

Some youth may join gangs and be forced to engage in acts of violence just to find a sense of belonging. Other children do not seem to have a safe place to go when they are feeling in danger or excluded. Unfortunately, gangs provide a sense of belonging to many young people, but unfortunately increase the violence greatly within our communities.

Homeless Youth

This is another problem that is put in this category of not belonging because if one does not have a shelter, a home, a place to be, then one is often ostracized within our communities. We have a significant homeless problem within our society. During the global economic crisis about 1.5 billion dollars were earmarked to assist the large population of unemployed and homeless.

We reside in the richest, most powerful country on Earth, and still we suffer from such basic safety concerns for our children as shelter and food. Homeless children not knowing where they will sleep each night or get their next meal is a much wider problem than we may care to acknowledge. The homeless population is probably larger than the available statistical information due to the rather invisible nature of this population who tend to try and keep their problems hidden due to embarrassment and a host of other reasons. Also, the problem is intertwined with many of the other problems facing our communities, such as unemployment and domestic violence.

Poverty and lack of available affordable housing is the largest cause of this basic survival need. Families cannot afford to live on minimum wages paid. Even a one-bedroom apartment is out of the reach of these individuals (let alone families.) To make matters worse, many of these are young people who also have incurred tremendous debt for educational/college costs, only to graduate and make low wages.

Eating healthy meals is almost impossible for these individuals, thus many are forced to subsist on high fat, high calorie inexpensive sources. Then we wonder why our country suffers from almost epidemic rates of obesity.

Children lacking shelter and basic needs are at higher risk for health problems, asthma, ear infections, stomach illnesses, and even speech problems. They are likely to experience hunger and even delayed development. Furthermore, they suffer from more mental health problems than most children including increased rates of anxiety, depression, and withdrawal (National Coalition for the Homeless, 2009, p. 3). The American Recovery Act of 2009 is trying to combat these issues. The basic needs of food, water, and shelter must be met if our children and communities are to be truly safe and thrive.

"Homeless youth are individuals under the age of eighteen who lack parental, foster, or institutional care. These young people are sometimes referred to as 'unaccompanied' youth."[17] The National Runaway Switchboard estimates that on any given night there are approximately 1.3 million homeless youth living unsupervised on the streets, in abandoned buildings, with friends or with strangers. Homeless youth are at a higher risk for physical abuse, sexual exploitation, mental health disabilities, substance abuse, and death. It is estimated that five thousand unaccompanied youth die each year as a result of assault, illness, or suicide.[18]

Furthermore, "data suggests that the current recession has yielded an increase in homeless and runaway youth. Between 2005 and 2008, the National Runaway Switchboard saw a 200 percent increase in calls from youth indicating economic reasons for running away from home. The Switchboard also reported an increase in the numbers of youth who were kicked out of their homes. A 2008 survey of school districts showed an increase in the number of homeless students" (NCSL, 2013, para. 2).

Although precise numbers of homeless youth are difficult to determine, in part due to movement of homeless individuals and inconsistencies in approaches to obtaining data, the numbers are quite alarming. Statistics suggest that as many as one out of every seven youth will run away, with 75 percent of these being females. Many of these are pregnant or gay, lesbian, bisexual, transgender, or queer young people. Many young homeless individuals are at high risk for being abused or forced into unwanted/illegal sexual situations.

Most of these young people also have dropped out of school, which hinders their chances for recovery even more (National Coalition for the Homeless, 2009).[19] Clearly, the basic needs of food, water, and shelter must be met if our children and communities are to be truly safe and thrive.

THE MISUNDERSTANDING OF MENTAL HEALTH ISSUES: FALLOUT FROM A DESENSITIZED POPULATION

Many children experience mental health problems because of the pressure they are under or because they are victims of bullying, violence, abuse, neglect, homelessness, or other problems. Believe it or not, often it is these individuals that are further victimized by the system and societal beliefs.

One should really ask, "Is this a problem more with society than with the individual?" The answer would be, "Yes, it is the individual showing symptoms (the identified patient), but what are the causes? We need to look much deeper into the misunderstanding of mental health issues."

Clearly, not every child develops problems, but that does not mean that the toxic conditions are not impacting every child. Just as some children are more susceptible to certain environmental toxins (molds), they can be deadly to some and only a nuisance to others, but not good for anyone.

MENTAL HEALTH FALLOUT

The fallout resulting in mental health issues impacts many individuals and is very costly both to each individual as well as society in terms of money, time away from school/work, mental anguish, and so forth. Here we will take a look at only a few of the major areas of mental illness that have been brought into the spotlight because of violence in our schools and other safety concerns with our youth.

The causes of mental illness are complex involving both individual factors as well as psychological, and environmental.

> Scientists currently think that, like heart disease and type 1 diabetes, mental illnesses are complex and probably result from a combination of genetic, environmental, psychological, and developmental factors. For instance, although [National Institute of Mental Health–]sponsored studies of twins and families suggest that genetics play a role in the development of some anxiety disorders, problems such as [posttraumatic stress disorder] are triggered by trauma. [20]

Additionally, according to the National Institute of Mental Health, scientists are also studying the effects of environmental factors including pollution, diet, and both physical and psychological stress. Clearly, researchers are aware of the interrelatedness of the issues within our ailing society that result in mental health fallout for many individuals.

Debunking a Common Myth

First of all, we must start out by debunking a myth regarding mental illness. Having a mental illness *does not* (automatically) make the individual a risk to our children or communities. Indeed, most people suffering from mental illness may be some of the most sensitive, least violent of our population.

According to R. Kinscherff, PhD, JD, senior associate at the National Center for Mental Health and Juvenile Justice and head of the American Psychological Association's Policy Review Task Force on the Predication and Prevention of Gun Violence: "Studies show that persons with severe and persistent major mental illness are not major contributors to gun violence" (Kinscherff, 2013, p. 3).

Many children are misunderstood because of a mental health label of autism spectrum disorder and Asperger's syndrome. Often, news reporters and others are quick to jump to conclusions that when violence does occur in a community or schools, it is because the child was diagnosed with a specific disorder. (Keep in mind the interaction issues involved with the safety concerns within our communities. Many children with mental illnesses, although often invisible, are targeted and become victims of bullying and not accepted within the schools and communities.[21])

Autism spectrum disorders are not fully understood as to their etiology. According to the National Institute of Mental Health, "many researchers are focusing on how various genes interact with each other and environmental factors to better understand how they increase the risk of this disorder. . . . This includes the air we breathe, the water we drink and bathe in, the food we eat, the medicines we take, and many other things that our bodies may come in contact with."[22]

Furthermore, the Centers for Disease Control and Prevention (CDC) have reported data from eleven communities within the United States. It seems that the rate of autism spectrum disorders is on the rise when compared with previous studies. Currently, approximately one out of every sixty-eight children may be suffering from an autism spectrum disorder with the rate of male children being four to five times higher than the risk for female children.[23]

An Alarming Rate of Anxiety Disorders

Anxiety disorders include a varied range of syndromes, such as posttraumatic stress disorder, panic disorder, and generalized anxiety disorder, which are quite common among the American population. According to the National Institute of Mental Health:

> Anxiety disorders affect about [forty] million American adults age [eighteen] years and older, and the adolescences *(sic)* ages [thirteen to eighteen] approximately 8 [percent] have an anxiety disorder with symptoms often starting

around the age of [six] years. Unfortunately only about 18 [percent] of these youth get assistance with their anxiety.[24]

The Common Occurrence of Depressive Disorders

Depression is often referred to as the common cold of mental illness and as with all mental illnesses, it is a very serious public health problem. Similar to the anxiety disorders, there is more than one type of depression that appears to be "caused by a combination of genetic, biological, environmental, and psychological factors."[25]

Additionally it is quite clear that depressive illnesses are disorders of the brain involving parts that influence mood, thinking, sleep, appetite, and behavior.[26]

Furthermore, depression seems to be possibly brought about by a synergistic interaction with genes and one's environment. It may also be triggered by trauma, loss of a loved one, a difficult relationship, or any stressful situation.[27]

Depression impacts about 6.7 percent of adults in the United States, and approximately 3.3% of youth between the ages of thirteen and eighteen have experienced a seriously debilitating depressive disorder.[28]

Suicidal Behavior

Under this section, it also is important to discuss suicidal behavior. Violence against the self, as suicide is sometimes called, can occur in youth. The educators and agency responders were quite correct to be worried about suicide as a serious safety risk. The CDC refers to suicide as a serious public health issue and that it impacts not only the individual but also has lasting effects upon parents, other students, and the communities (CDC, September, 9, 2014).[29]

All suicides are tragic, since help is available for even the most difficult cases. Youth suicides, because of the age of the victims, are even more heartbreaking and unfortunately on the rise. The following statistics from the CDC can put this serious issue into perspective: (CDC, September, 9, 2014)[30]

- "For youth between the ages of [ten and twenty-four], suicide is the third leading cause of death. It results in approximately 4,600 lives lost each year. The top three methods used in suicides of young people include firearm (45%), suffocation (40%), and poisoning (8%)". (CDC, September, 9, 2014)
- A nationwide survey of youth in grades nine to twelve in public and private schools in the United States found that 16 percent of students reported seriously considering suicide, 13 percent reported creating a plan,

and 8 percent reporting trying to take their own life in the twelve months preceding the survey.

- Each year, approximately 157,000 youth between the ages of ten and twenty-four receive medical care for self-inflicted injuries at emergency departments across the United States. Suicide affects all youth, but some groups are at higher risk than others.
- Boys are more likely than girls to die from suicide. Of the reported suicides in the ten to twenty-four age group, 81 percent of the deaths were males and 19 percent were females. Girls, however, are more likely to report attempting suicide than boys.
- Cultural variations in suicide rates also exist, with Native American/Alaskan Native youth having the highest rates of suicide related fatalities. A nationwide survey of youth in grades nine to twelve in public and private schools in the United States found Hispanic youth were more likely to report attempting suicide than their black and white, non-Hispanic peers (CDC, September, 9, 2014).

The Cases When Mental Health Problems Pose a Serious Danger to Others

This section began with mental health issues by discussing the misunderstanding and fear that many people have around those suffering from mental illness. There are really not that many dangerous individuals out there. Most of our community members are good and humane people, including those that may suffer from mental illness at some point in their lives.

Nonetheless, in some cases there are individuals that are quite dangerous. Unfortunately, these are also the individuals who are less well understood, with fewer effective treatment options or availability of treatment. Often, these individuals have shown early symptoms, but are not effectively treated and end up in the prison systems utilizing a punishment approach with very high recidivism rates.

Some individuals may become dangerous during psychotic episodes when the individual cannot distinguish between reality and fantasy. Thus he/she may believe and act upon delusions and hallucinations, putting the individual and others at serious risk.

Other sometimes dangerous individuals may have a form of psychopathy or a pattern of deceitful, callous, manipulative, and remorseless behavior (Mash and Wolfe, 2013, p. 488). For example, this grouping will include psychopaths and sociopaths in our society.

Upon analyzing the problems of conduct with children and adults, it becomes clear that there is no one simple answer, as with other forms of mental illness there are hosts of interacting influences. Research reported in Mash and Wolfe (2013) indicates that the causes of conduct problems are complex and may involve genetic risks, prenatal and birth complications, neurobiological influences, the social and cognitive abilities of the child, and family environmental issues. Additionally the surrounding community and school may play a part along with exposure to media violence and cultural factors (pp. 182-191).

According to Mash and Wolfe:

> There indeed can be possible genetic risk and prenatal and birth complications that can put the child more at risk for developing conduct problems/disorders. Also environmental factors such as exposure to lead paint and individual neuro-biological differences including, functional and structural deficits in the pre-frontal cortex, difficult temperament, insecure attachment in infancy.
>
> Additionally if the child grows up in a family with antisocial values, behaviors or disorders of the sort including antisocial personality disorder, substance abuse, marital problems, low socioeconomic levels, single parent households, mothers with low levels of education and access to weapons within the household there is a possible risk, but not necessarily causal in nature.

Additionally, schools are a large part of the lives of children from about age five years on (or even earlier with many children attending day care and preschools). When children are rejected by their peers, bullied, or associated with other children with deviation, this may lead some children down paths of violence.

When children see schools as places of punishment and places where they are not able to succeed, and do not feel a part of the school community, there too may be problems brewing. When children have some combination of these factors, they are more at risk for developing conduct/behavioral problems which tend to run a course of becoming more severe over time without intervention.

A child may begin with oppositional defiant disorder and develop as he/she ages into more serious conduct problems where a diagnosis of conduct disorder would be warranted. Here, too, conduct disorders are one of the diagnoses with the least effective treatment course, not because these children are hopeless, but because the factors are many and interventions may need to be larger in scope and ongoing. Indeed, these are problems not only of the child, but the child is merely exhibiting symptoms of a sick society, a sick climate. This truly is a diagnosis that should not be looked at as an individual problem but a true public health risk.

Certainly, all children go through times or phases when they are more negative, less cooperative than other times. The children with oppositional defiant disorder and the more severe conduct disorder truly are hurting others and lacking in social consciousness. They may seem callous and unemotional and may have difficulty keeping friends. They may act more impulsively without forethought, blame others, and engage in more risky behaviors (Mash and Wolfe, 2013).

And some are terrorists who may have been indoctrinated, brainwashed into believing that others are out to get them. Thus, they have been programmed and taught to be delusional, and their behaviors can be quite violent as we have seen in many instances of terrorism around the globe.

Consequently, many individuals develop serious permanent yet invisible psychological scars. Such afflictions may affect future prospects in education and employment, lead to substantial economic costs in terms of medical treatment and loss of wages, and result in physical and emotional costs to individuals.

Although we are probably safer than we have been from all of the precautions that have been identified and developed over the years, we still have much work to do because of the changing nature of the safety concerns, which of course is what this book is all about. The next section presents a discussion of what our current needs are to develop a safer community for our children and for us all.

NOTES

1. Retrieved 12/8/14 from http://www.fbi.gov/about-us/cjis/ucr/hate-crime/2012/resource-pages/about-hate-crime/abouthatecrime_final
2. www.bullyingstatistics.org.
3. www.bullyingstatistics.org.
4. Retrieved 12/8/14 from http://www.bullyingstatistics.org/content/school-bullying-statistics.html
5. www.bullyingstatistics.org.
6. Centers for Disease Control and Prevention, 2014, paragraph 1 from http://www.cdc.gov/healthyyouth/alcoholdrug/.
7. Drugabuse.gov, from http://www.drugabuse.gov/publications/drugfacts/high-school-youth-trends.
8. Retrieved from http://www.drugabuse.gov/publications/drugfacts/high-school-youth-trends.
9. Retrieved from http://www.drugabuse.gov/publications/drugfacts/high-school-youth-trends.
10. Retrieved from http://www.drugabuse.gov/publications/drugfacts/high-school-youth-trends.
11. Retrieved from http://www.drugabuse.gov/publications/drugfacts/high-school-youth-trends.
12. World Health Organization, 2006.
13. World Health Organization, 2006.
14. World Health Organization, 2006.
15. World Health Organization, 2006.
16. U.S. Bureau of the Census, Income, Poverty, and Health Insurance Coverage in the United States: 2010, Report P60, n. 238, Table B-2, pp. 68–73.
17. Retrieved 12/7/14 from http://nationalhomeless.org/wp-content/uploads/2014/06/youth-Fact-Sheet.pdf Published by the National Coalition for the Homeless, June 2008.
18. National Coalition for the Homeless, 2009, p. 3.
19. Retrieved June 16, 2014, from http://www.ncsl.org/research/human-services/homeless-and-runaway-youth.aspx#_ednref1.

20. Retrieved August 3, 2014, from http://www.nimh.nih.gov/health/topics/anxiety-disorders/index.shtml.

21. Retrieved August 3, 2014, from http://www.nimh.nih.gov/health/topics/autism-spectrum-disorders-asd/index.shtml.

22. Retrieved August 3, 2014, from http://www.nimh.nih.gov/health/topics/autism-spectrum-disorders-asd/index.shtml.

23. Retrieved August 3, 2014, from http://www.nimh.nih.gov/health/topics/autism-spectrum-disorders-asd/index.shtml.

24. Retrieved August 3, 2014, from http://www.nimh.nih.gov/health/topics/anxiety-disorders/index.shtml#part4.

25. Retrieved August 3, 2014, from http://www.nimh.nih.gov/health/topics/depression/index.shtml.

26. Retrieved August 3, 2014, from http://www.nimh.nih.gov/health/topics/depression/index.shtml.

27. Retrieved August 3, 2014, from http://www.nimh.nih.gov/health/topics/depression/index.shtml.

28. Retrieved 12/13/14 from http://www.nimh.nih.gov/health/topics/depression/index.shtml.

29. Retrieved 12/13/1/4 from http://www.cdc.gov/violenceprevention/suicide/

30. Retrieved 12/13/1/4 from http://www.cdc.gov/violenceprevention/suicide/

Part IV

Working Together: Developing Safer Climates for Our Children

By working together from a multidisciplinary, research-based approach, we can manage the complexity of the issues involved to make our schools and communities safer for our children and for us all.

Chapter 10

So, Now What? Who's in Charge Anyway? What Do We Need? What Do We Do Next?

There can be no keener revelation of a society's soul than the way in which it treats its children.
–Nelson Mandela

It would be great if there was a quick and easy solution to all the safety concerns that plague our schools and communities. It seems to bring up even more questions now, but these questions will lead us in the direction of developing safer schools and communities. Would it not be wonderful if we could just list ten or twelve cookbook solutions that would protect us from the toxic conditions that jeopardize our children? Sorry, we already know it is not that simple, but this book will present major problematic queries that contribute and exacerbate the identified safety issues, and yes we can make changes in these areas.

WHO'S IN CHARGE?

The first question that needs to be answered is, "Who's in charge?" Because of the complexity and interdisciplinary nature of the issues involved with youth safety and safe schools, it is confusing as to who is and/or who should be in charge. Many boundaries are crossed when the safety of children is in jeopardy at the local community and state levels, as well as the national and even international levels, as one can see from the research cited within this book. Thus it involves the youth, their parents, school personnel, police, the Federal Bureau of Investigation, Homeland Security, Department of Education, National Institute of Mental Health, the Centers for Disease Control and Prevention, and even the World Health Organization to fully understand the issues at hand and the short- and long-term ramifications.

All of these professional groupings are made up of knowledgeable and skilled "experts" within their respective fields, but they do not always work well in conjunction with one another. Research funding is available for some, but not for others, and the competition for funding is aggressive, possibly contributing to the silo effect we often see particularly within institutions of higher education (including our Research 1 institutions) within the United States. The silo effect has negative impacts due to a lack of collaboration, competition between researchers, and isolation.

To highlight this problem, many related fields including psychology, criminal justice, education, social work, public health, and related fields are researching these very safety problems to help understand the issues, causes, impacts, and potential interventions. However, most often the research is not conducted in an interdisciplinary manner.

Even when the Federal Bureau of Investigation works in conjunction with the Department of Education and consulting psychologists, the report comes through reading more as a police control issue rather than effective preventative measures and intervention based upon research for the related experts. (It seems more of how our prisons work under a model of punishment instead of rehabilitation.)

Our justice system is used to taking control and being in control, and no doubt this is needed in some situations, but the situations where our children's safety is at risk is complex and often needs more collaboration. (We do not need to go in with full riot gear to lower elementary school classrooms, either scaring the children and creating thoughts that such safety violations are likely to happen in our schools, or unfortunately even reinforcing the use of weapons and force in the very impressionable young minds of some children.)

Thus, the question of who is in charge needs to be addressed from a team approach based upon the issues at hand and the research available. It requires a team approach involving experts form the related disciplines with equal input.

Ultimately, there will need to be a team collaboration, which has the final say. This group will need to be made up of interdisciplinary experts capable of grasping the research concepts from many fields and acting responsibly and in a timely manner in critical situations. Researchers and professionals from the fields of psychology, public health, criminal justice, sociology, and education will need to have strong voices along with the first responders who ultimately need to protect our communities.

Ongoing research, training, discussions, and reflections must be conducted in a collaborative and cooperative manner to bridge the gap that tends to occur with our present system. Research in areas is so very often not applied when dealing with safety concerns. It is ignored because of conflicting results waiting for the final undisputable data, which will never come because of the complexity and changing nature of our world. This is so perplexing and frustrating, just as it was for many years when medical professions knew there was a strong correlation between smoking and lung cancer, but the public was not warned or protected until many years later, partially due to the very strong political lobby of the tobacco industry.

The issues of lack of cooperation and greed can clearly be seen in this example, just as we are seeing today with the violence in the gaming and media industries. Psychologist Paul Ekman (2008), when discussing the nature of compassion with the Dali Lama, believes that: "Technology allows us to kill at such a distance, we do not even see the person we are killing. . . . Seeing the suffering we are inflicting has restrained at least some people from killing, but now we do not even see the harm. It makes it much more dangerous" (p. 151).

This makes people much more desensitized and removed from the violence and the resulting suffering. As stated previously, even playing games does change the brain, at least for a period of time in people. Critics will say well, how do we know it changes the brains of everyone? Clearly, this is a question that can never be answered without testing each and every individual in the world. It makes much more sense to make policies on the side of reasonable doubt and be safe.

Thus, being a member on this interdisciplinary research and policymaking team would not be a job for the faint of heart; the decision-making process involves the lives of our youth and communities. Nationally, there would be a team of overseers, with state and local teams addressing the more regional and home-based issues. Thus, the question "Who is in charge?" is a critical one.

WHAT DO WE NEED?

The next question involves our current needs. Some of what we need is already in place; thus the infrastructure for making our schools and communities safer for our children is in place, but some updating, tweaking, reorganization, and collaboration among and between involved organizations is in order.

Taking a look at the updating needed, here are some unassailable recommendations that will go a long way to making our schools and communities safer places: meeting the basic needs and resolving the inequities, and assuring adequate funding is available and well managed.

First and foremost, we need to meet the basic needs of our children and all members of our communities. In order to do this, adequate funding must be made available and equally importantly our political system must work together, not against one another.

- The lack of a sense of community felt by those who are new to our country or those who are different in some ways and bullied or ostracized is problematic and against our country's core values. This most definitively creates situations where many people feel resentful, retaliatory, anxious, depressed, and at times even hopeless. It is very difficult for many Americans to understand the horrors that many refugees have experienced, but here is where a humanitarian nature must come into play, for we are a nation of caring individuals.
- Likewise, the economic crisis experienced worldwide over the last several years has left many homeless or without adequate nourishment or clothing. This too exacerbates safety problems within our society.
- Although the laws and infrastructure are well in place to try and protect children from abuse and neglect, we can improve these issues too. Due to such concerns as not wanting to get involved, fear of reporting, and the red tape that often ensues, children may fall between the cracks and not receive the help they need.
- The inequities that so many of our citizens experience, within our schools, with their salaries and so forth, need to be a top priority within our country. It is not just a problem of the "haves and the have nots" or the eroding middle class within our society. It really is a form of continued discrimination that is unlawful and downright wrong. We can do much better in this area.

The reader may notice that the categories are beginning to overlap due to the interconnected nature of the problems. The issue of inequity for example falls within both the meeting of basic needs and the next section on challenging outdated concepts.

OUTDATED IDEAS NEED TO BE CHALLENGED

- Outdated ideas include such opinions as: "If it was good enough for me, it's good enough for the children." Ill-informed citizens need to be made aware of the research underpinning the safety concerns within our society. Our communities and schools have changed: what may once have been adequate no longer is due to the complexity of our world.
- Discrimination of any form must be confronted. Some forms are quite subtle since laws have been established for many years now protecting the rights of all individuals despite one's race, gender, religious beliefs, and so forth. Nonetheless, inequities still are prevalent within our communities. Individualism is out of balance.

New laws must be developed based upon our changing culture. For example, the issue of gun control is important to discuss here. The developing culture of violence we discussed in previous chapters is fueled by our weapon/gun mentality.

We live in a very different world than our forefathers back in the 1780s and early 1790s when the Bill of Rights first went into effect. The lawmakers at this time understood their culture well and made the best attempts to protect the people and their rights. (Of course, some made laws that did not respect the rights of individuals, for example the laws that permitted slavery within some states.)

Protecting the rights and freedoms of all people equally is paramount in the United States, but part of protecting people's rights and freedoms changes over the years and our country has made remarkable progress over the last more than two hundred years. Thus laws decidedly need updating as our world changes to continue to protect the lives and safety of all our citizens.

Back in the late 1700s, the colonies were engaged in a war against England to win our freedom. These were dangerous times; communities were much more rural with houses fewer and farther between. Neighbors were less able to come to the aid of their community members, wild animals were prevalent, and farmers needed to be able to protect their livestock, indeed their lives depended upon it.

People needed to hunt to get their next meal on the table. Today, we merely go to the many grocery stores carrying fresh meats, fruits, and vegetables from around the world.

For the most part, this is not our world any longer: we have the strongest military in the world, each state has its own state police force, and each community is protected by their local police and fire departments. These individuals are well trained; they take their jobs seriously and with few exceptions do an excellent job of protecting our citizens.

R. Kinscherff, PhD, JD, senior associate at the National Center for Mental Health and Juvenile Justice and head of the American Psychological Association's Policy Review Task Force on the Predication and Prevention of Gun Violence[1] sees this issue of gun violence as needing "a broad public health approach focused on both prevention and intervention" (p. 3).

Dr. Kinscherff reports that gun ownership appears to vary greatly by region. He asserts that over the last fifteen years, the general crime rate has been declining, including gun use as well as the number of households in which someone possesses a gun (p. 3). This is hopeful; however, the more specific information included in this report is alarming and indicates that most gun deaths are by suicide and that gun violence disproportionally impacts people of color, low socioeconomic status, and disenfranchised populations.

Our current needs within our country are quite different than when the second amendment to the Bill of Rights was written in Congress on March 4, 1789. This modification, which is more than two hundred years old now, states, "a well-regulated Militia, being necessary to the security of the free State, the right of the people to bear Arms, shall not be infringed." Well, we have a very well-regulated militia, but we are not the Minutemen of Lexington, drinking it up in the taverns along Massachusetts Avenue, knowing that they indeed will be involved in a fight for their lives and their freedom.

Our first responders and our military are well-trained professionals that protect us today. Our actions should not put these brave men and women in jeopardy. Their lives are often put in jeopardy by deviant individuals who can buy deadly weapons at local stores without any training, and unfortunately many children have easy access to weapons within their homes, but lack the cognitive development to grasp the seriousness and permanence of the effects that these weapons cause. Our world has changed; no longer does owning a gun protect us, but indeed it may make us less safe.

A REBALANCING OF THE MANY STRESSORS WITHIN OUR SOCIETY

Parents and community members are under more pressures today than ever before, including the financial woes of the past several years with many out of work, losing their homes, while trying to cope with their aging parents, college expenses, and needs of their children.

Many from this generation will be unable to retire when they reach retirement age. People are living longer than ever before, the need for medical and other benefits are great, and many individuals had their retirement funds depleted during the economic crisis. It also is not unusual to hear that the expectations at work have been increasing as businesses try to stay competitive with fewer employees. Job security is much less secure with more expectations on performance.

The pressure on our children has increased greatly as well. Kids are forced to grow up too fast, but they are not taught how to handle stressful situations or responsibility. Some are overly scheduled in activities with little free time to relax and learn to think for themselves. Others are undersupervised and may become involved with activities that include brainless hours of watching television, gaming, or being plugged into their electronic peers. Some may become involved with gangs, drugs, and other unsavory activities in an attempt to find where they belong and reduce boredom (which can also be quite stressful in a different way).

Many call our young population the "entitled generation," where they expect to be able to have whatever they want. Certainly, parents want to give their children many of the pleasures they experienced as children and even more than their parents were able to provide. This is human nature in some ways, and it is possibly a reaction to the guilt may parents feel for the need for both parents to work and being less available to their children due to highly stressful career demands.

It can be a rude awakening when our youth realize they are in a highly competitive, stressful world where they must compete for grades, excel in sports or other activities that can earn them a scholarship, all while trying to fit in with their peers and cope with their changing bodies and raging hormones during the already stressful teenage years. Furthermore, it can be difficult for our young people as they get caught up in this stressful cycle of pressure from their parents, their teachers, and their peers.

When they become young adults, they must cope with costly college loans, car loans, and high rents which are really getting out of control. Young people from other thriving countries do not experience the incredible costs associated with getting a college degree to the extent in the United States. Indeed in many countries, the cost of college and even graduate school may be covered for those motivated, bright young people wanting to pursue a career in education for example.

The stressful impacts often leave our young with issues of denial, distortions, disillusionment, and helplessness. Some will abuse drugs or alcohol, or fall prey to any number of the safety concerns discussed. Many will experience mental illness, some will act out in anger or retaliation, others will become victims, and thus the downward cycle continues.

A BALANCE OF ETHICS IS ESSENTIAL

- A strong sense of ethical responsibility is out of equilibrium when businesses, advertising, media, policymakers, and so forth put the issue of

economics above the value of our children. The balance will be reestab-
lished when we see changes to do what is right and best for our children,
not what is least expensive, not what will make someone the most profit,
and not what is going to get one ahead politically.
- A balance between freedom and rights with a strong ethic of responsibility
  and caring for the self and community members is what is needed to
  develop a safer community. Such a culture requires responsibility to be
  learned over time, not suddenly plunging our youth into it as so many are
  when they graduate from high school or college today.

Throughout their earlier school years, they can be overly supervised and
controlled to the point they do not know how to handle the responsibilities
that are not earned in our culture, but attained by one's chronological age.
(For example, many sixteen-year-olds are not responsible enough to safely
drive, even when they are quite capable and skillful with the process of
driving.)

The expectation of many youth is one of entitlement without having
earned and/or being cognitively developed enough to manage the rights and
privileges that go along with gaining access to more mature undertakings.
Thus, we have a need to rebalance the excessiveness we see within our
society; indeed, there is too much access to everything technologically, including weapons and so forth. Most alarmingly, it is these potentially harmful things that, when used inappropriately or excessively, may create safety
problems for our children and ourselves.

The issues of rights and freedoms bring to mind other imbalances as well
between our, at times, overly permissive environments coupled with an overly restrictive authoritarian rule. Either extreme may increase our safety concerns for our children and teens, with taking increased risks resulting in, for
example, pregnancies, even though condoms are given out. The expectations
are to take risks as teens. It is this progression that is in need of checks and
balances.

MORE OPTIMISM NEEDED

The rebalancing of our cultural mindset to be more on the realistic, yet
optimistic side is very important. There are many aspects of our environments that we cannot control, at least not yet. So far we are not able to
prevent tornadoes, but we do not need to be paralyzed by fear either. We can
make choices to ensure the safety of our children by choosing to have the
needed shelters in place.

Although there are many things we have learned from the devastation and
anguish of September 11, 2001, there is another one we all must learn and

that is that we cannot live in fear. Clearly, after reading this book, we live in a dangerous world, but there are many things we can do to prevent and cope with these concerns. Optimism and hope is essential for us to be able to see possibilities, use our creativity to respond to problems, and believe that we are all (at least most of us) capable of working together.

I am not talking about putting on rose-colored glasses or putting our heads in the sand; I am talking about looking realistically and creatively at the issues, and hopefully dealing with the concerns. In order to do this, we do have to realize that we have a choice in how we think. Whether you realize it or not, we each have the ability to choose to respond differently to situations, and this can be learned behavior as suggested by Martin Seligman (1990, 1998, 2006, 2011). Seligman, after years of research, has even developed programs where this learned optimism and resilience can be implemented with children. However, here again we see the disconnect between research and policies.

Thinking in a more optimistic manner and developing resilience does not mean that we forget past incidents, but that we seek positive, helpful solutions, not resentment, hatred, and retaliation. This, too, can start with our young in our schools by working to develop healthy climates in our schools that teach optimism, resilience, respect for all living beings, and cooperation and collaboration on not only a school, community, and national basis, but on a global basis.

As discussed, the safety concerns our youth face are not just limited to our local school and communities, although there certainly are problems there too. But unfortunately many children are taught resentment and to hold on to anger and even taught to retaliate as discussed by Ekman (2008) and the Dalai Lama (p. 194).

Obviously, we cannot and should not forget the past, but we can respond in an intelligent manner and differently than through more acts of violence. Thus the important safety message is not to forget the past, but not hold on to resentment either (Ekman, p. 195).

Ekman (2008) expressed his belief that we do have a reason to hope. He gave the example of when people see on the news images and stories of people suffering even in faraway places from a tsunami or hurricane, so many people are quick to respond to help (p. 196). He also believes that people have a moral responsibility to help and when they do so it helps the helpers to not only feel a sense of happiness and satisfaction, but to gain knowledge that he/she can overcome, to prevent becoming overwhelmed and discouraged, indeed to gain confidence and courage. This, too, gives us great hope and we know that most of the people in the world are good, moral, and caring people. Together, we can deal with the problems and by together I mean within our schools our communities, our nation, and our world. Our problems do not occur in isolation.

The best explanation of this interrelatedness comes from an unlikely source: the spiritual leader of the Tibetan people, the Dalai Lama. He believes there is a need for global thinking which must involve the understanding that we are all interconnected. With global thinking, many of the world's problems may be avoided, including social and political problems and this is a long term ongoing process. He and Ekman (2008) stress the need for all scientists to collaborate with one another (rather than negatively competing), and develop a sense of internationalism where each nation works together (p. 190). Ekman (2008) describes how there can be a positive type of competition and a negative type (p. 190).

SO WHAT'S NEXT?

The next steps need to include:

- Ongoing research on a cooperative, collaborative, interdisciplinary, and global basis. Developing a team approach to bridge the gap between research fields and the appropriate application of this knowledge into our schools and communities is critical. It is imperative to work together in a cooperative and collaborative manner to get the needed research-based policies, procedures, training, shelters, and equipment in place for each child.
- Developing a more positive sense of climate within our schools, communities, and country where all people feel a sense of belonging and responsibility. This needs to be a culture where violence, bullying, and other forms of safety problems are not tolerated or ignored.

To accomplish these steps teachers need to be held in the highest esteem for what they do for our children and communities. Furthermore, the most academically capable students need to be encouraged to become teachers, provided with the necessary advanced education and skills, along with monetary compensation deserved by this essential profession and the needed time to do their best work. Passivity on the part of school or community personnel that allows for the cycle of toxicity to continue will not be tolerated. One statistic which speaks to this unfortunate issue involves school bullying where in about 85 percent of bullying cases, no intervention or effort is made by a teacher or administration member of the school to stop the bullying from taking place (bullyingstatistics.org). However, with a more active approach, the number of students that live in fear of being bullied should decrease.

The same holds true for individuals labeled with a mental health issue. Many potential dynamics and influences of these disorders can be prevented, alleviated, mitigated, or have effective interventions if identified; as with any other problem, ongoing research is critical. For example, to reduce factors that increase risk of suicide, we must reduce the risk factors as previously discussed and increase factors that promote resilience (i.e., protective factors).[2]

Ideally, prevention addresses all levels of influence: individual, relationship, community, and societal. Effective prevention strategies are needed to promote awareness of suicide and encourage a commitment to social change.

Curriculum changes in our schools should all be based upon research and include:

- Helping children develop better ways of coping: to learn to be realistic, yet optimistic, to develop resiliency, confidence, and solid coping skills to deal with stress.
- Assisting children to learn to be respectful of all living beings and to appreciate the diversity.
- Teaching children to learn healthy ways of relaxing and coping with everyday stressors.
- Well-organized and accessible after-school programs that provide equal access to all children. These should involve not only extracurricular academic activities such as enrichment programs and tutoring, but also sports and healthy recreation and socialization.
- Funding for access to higher education for our deserving young people is paramount. Of course, this also needs to be accessible to all deserving young people who are motivated to work hard and make a difference for the better to our communities.

Standardized testing cannot be the only way that these deserving young people are awarded since as we know from *Hidden Dangers* (Gunzelmann, 2008, 2011) so many of our most talented young people are inadvertently weeded out by the mistaken reliance on this form of testing.

Performance over time is a much better motivator and indicator of future performance. However, with this stated, we also must be careful to give young people opportunity who have more recently, yet sincerely made changes to a new path in a committed and responsible manner.

Additionally our schools must have:

- Identified safe people and places to go when threatened. Young people struggling with harassment, bullying, gender, racial, or any other issue should have people they are confortable talking with and know how to reach in case of emergency. Cutting down on the positions of school counselors and school psychologists when the need is rising is another penny wise/pound foolish policy.
- Safe rooms and shelters in case of natural or manmade disasters.

As defined by the Federal Emergency Management Agency (FEMA; 2008), "A safe room is a hardened structure specifically designed to meet the FEMA criteria and provide 'near-absolute protection' in extreme weather events, including tornadoes and hurricanes. Near-absolute protection means that, based on our current knowledge of tornadoes and hurricanes, the occupants of a safe room built in accordance with FEMA guidance will have a very high probability of being protected from injury or death."

Such shelters must be adequate and safely built to the specifications of needs within the specific areas. For example, tsunamis may not occur in Ohio, but tornado shelters should be available and accessible to everyone in this locality. Funding must be made available before any more children are lost to preventable disasters. Safe rooms must be large enough and have adequate supplies to safely protect all occupants.

- Additionally, although FEMA has preparedness booklets for what to do in case of such natural disasters as earthquakes and tornadoes, a very real problem is that there is a huge gap between being ready on paper and being ready for the reality of such disasters. When an emergency strikes, there is little time to refer to paper references. Adults should be mindful and practice these procedures, but without needlessly traumatizing the students.
- Along these same lines, the continued research in weather detection and alert systems should continue to be funded and ongoing. Collaboration with the technological experts here is vital as well.
- Clearly all our schools and buildings should be free from environmental hazards, some of which may not show up as health hazards until many years later, as in the cases of asbestos-related illnesses and many other health issues.
- Last but certainly not least, I mention the need for transparent, ethical, research-based and interdisciplinary teams to oversee the development and maintenance of the implementation of needs.

Just putting a Band-Aid on these problems, as has been done to date, and hoping the safety concerns, disasters, and crises were either isolated incidents or that they will eventually heal up and disappear is naive and irresponsible. Such approaches only contribute more to the problems we are seeing in our schools and communities. Undoubtedly these problems need direct, intensive, sustained, research-based interventions from a coordinated team-centered approach. Only then will we have thriving and safer communities and schools for our children and for us all. Only then can we say we are fully attending to the interdisciplinary responsibility of our time.

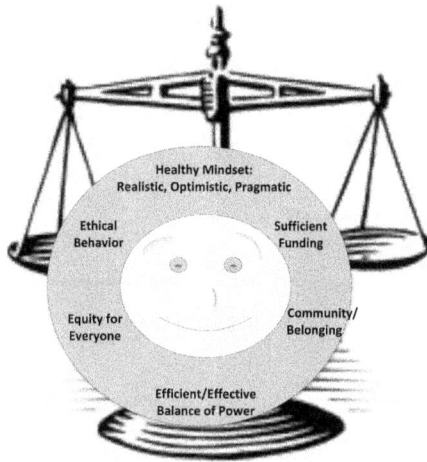

NOTES

1. December 2013, p. 3, *New England Psychologists*.
2. Retrieved July 24, 2014, from http://www.cdc.gov/violenceprevention/suicide/.

References and Suggested Readings

Anderson, C. A. (2003). Violent video games: Myths, facts and unanswered questions. *Psychological Science Agenda.* http://www.apa.org/science/about/psa/2003/10/anderson.aspx.

Anderson, C. A., and Bushman, B. J. (2001). Effects of violent video games on aggressive behavior, aggressive cognition, aggressive affect, physiological arousal, and prosocial behavior: A meta-analytical review of the scientific literature. *Psychological Science,* 12(5), 353–359.

Annan, K. (2001). *The Nobel lecture given by the Nobel prize laureate 2001, Kofi A. Annan.* (Oslo, December 10, 2001).

Armstrong, 2012.

Bandura, A., Ross, D., and Ross, S. A. (1963). Imitation of film mediated aggressive models. *Journal of Abnormal and Social Psychology,* 66(1): 3–11.

Bandura, A. (1965). Influence of models' reinforcement contingencies on the acquisition of imitative responses. *Journal of Personality and Social Psychology,* 1, 589–595.

Bandura, A. (1977). *Social Learning Theory.* New York: General Learning Press.

Black, S. (2004). Safe schools don't need zero tolerance. *Education Digest,* 70(2), 27–31.

Boeree, G. C. (2006). The History of Psychology (I-IV). Retrieved 12/14/15 from [http://www.ship.edu/%7Ecgboeree/historyofpsych.html]

Bonnie, Richard J., and O'Connell, Mary Ellen (eds.). (2004). *Reducing underage drinking: A collective responsibility.* Washington, DC: The National Academies Press.

Brazelton, T. B., and Greenspan, S. I. (2000). *The irreducible needs of children: What every child must have to grow, learn, and flourish.* Cambridge, MA: Perseus.

Brook, S., Lazarus, P., and Jimerson, S. (2002). *Creating nurturing classroom environments: Fostering hope and resilience as an antidote to violence.* Best Practices in School Crisis Prevention and Intervention. National Association of School Psychologists.

Brookmeyer, Fanti, and Henrich 2006; Goldstein, Young, and Boyd 2008. In NCES Indicators of School Crime and Violence: 2013 retrieved 7/24/14 from http://nces.ed.gov/programs/crimeindicators/crimeindicators2013/index.asp

Brown, Brene. Brainy Quotes. Retrieved from http://www.brainyquote.com/quotes/keywords/belonging.html#AGvzCALu3lrkfFEW.99.

Brumfield, K. (May 20, 2014) Moore, Oklahoma, looks back on tornado that killed 24 one year ago. CNN. Retrieved 12/14/5/14 from http://www.cnn.com/2014/05/20/us/oklahoma-moore-tornado-anniversary /

Bushman, B. J. & Anderson, C. A. Media violence and the American public: Scientific facts versus media misinformation. *American Psychologist,* Vol 56(6-7), Jun-Jul, 2001. pp. 477-489 US: American Psychological Association.

Bushman, B. J. & Anderson, C. A. (2002) Violent video games and hostile expectations: A test of the general aggression model. *PSBS*, Vol. 28, No. 12 December 2002, 1679-1686.

Bushman, B. J. & Anderson, C. A. (2009). Comfortably numb: Desensitizing effects of violent media on helping others. *Psychological Science*, 21(3), 273-277.

Bushman, B. J. & Gibson, B. (2011). Violent video games cause an increase in aggression long after the game has been turned off. *Social Psychological and Personality Science* 2:29. Originally published online August 11, 2010 http://spp.sagepub.com/content/2/1/29.

Cacioppo, J. T., Hawkley, L. C., Norman, G. J., and Berntson, G. G. (2011). Social isolation. *Annals of New York Academy of Sciences*, 1231(1), 17–22.

Centers for Disease Control and Prevention. Understanding school violence. Retrieved April 18, 2010 from www.cdc.gov/violenceprevention.

Centers for Disease Control and Prevention. (2012).

Centers for Disease Control and Prevention. (2013a). Retrieved June 16, 2014, from www.cdc. gov/acohol.fact-sheet/underage-drinking.htm.

Centers for Disease Control and Prevention. (2013b). Retrieved June 16, 2014, from http:// www.cdc.gov/std/stats/STI-Estimates-Fact-Sheet-Feb-2013.pdf.

Centers for Disease Control and Prevention. (2014).

Connell, D., and Gunzelmann, B. (2004). The new gender gap: Why are so many boys floundering while so many girls are soaring? *Instructor* 113(6), 14–17.

Cottle, T. (2001) *At peril: Stories of injustices*. Amherst: University of Massachusetts Press.

Darling-Hammond, L. (May 21, 2007). "Evaluating 'No Child Left Behind'" Retrieved 12/7/14 from http://www.forumforeducation.org/publications/articles/evaluating-no-child-left-behind.

Dillon, A. (May 24, 2004). "Education in Plato's Republic," presented at the Santa Clara University Student Ethics Research Conference. Retrieved August 15, 2007 from http:// www.scu.edu/ethics/publications/submitted/dillon/education_pla...

Djordjevic, J., Djordjevic, A., Adzic, M., & Radojcic, M. B. Neuropsychobiology, 2012. Effects of chronic social isolation on Wistar rat behavior and brain plasticity markers.

Ekman, P. (ed). (2008). *Emotional awareness: A conversation between the Dalai Lama and Paul Ekman, Ph.D.* New York: Holt.

Elkind, D. (1988). *The hurried child.* Reading, MA: Perseus Publishing.

Elkind, D. (2001). *The hurried child* (3rd ed.). Cambridge, MA: DeCapo Press.

Farberman, R. (2006). Zero tolerance policies can have unintended effects, APA report finds. *Monitor on Psychology*, 37(9), 27.

Federal Bureau of Investigation. (2012). Uniform Crime Reports. 2012 Hate Crime Statistics. Washington, DC. Retrieved 12/8/14 from http://www.fbi.gov/about-us/cjis/ucr/hate-crime/ 2012/resource-pages/about-hate-crime/abouthatecrime_final

Federal Emergency Management Agency. (2008). Retrieved August 17, 2013, from http:// www.fema.gov/safe-rooms.

Federal Emergency Management Agency. Retrieved August 17, 2013, from http:// www.disastersrus.org/emtools/earthquakes/fema-526.pdf.

Finkelhor, D., Turner, H., Ormrod, R., Hambly, S., and Krake, K. (October 2009). Children's exposure to violence: A comprehensive national survey. OJJDP National Survey of Children's Exposure to Violence. Retrieved April 20, 2010, from http://www.ncjrs.gov/ pdffiles1/ojjdp/227744.pdf.

Gardner, H. (1991). *The unschooled mind: How children think and how schools should teach.* New York: Basic Books.

Gardner, H., Csikszentmihalyi, M., and Damon, W. (2001). *Good work: When excellence and ethics meet.* New York: Basic Books.

Gentile, D. A., and Anderson, C. A. (2003). Violence hazard. In Douglas A. Gentile, ed. *Media violence and children: A complete guide for parents and professionals.* New York: Praeger.

Glew, G., Fan, M., Katon, W., Rivara, F., and Kernic, M. (2005). Bullies, victims, and their feelings about school. *Archives of Pediatrics and Adolescent Medicine*, 159(11), 1004–1085.

Global Green USA. (2006). Green Schools Initiative. Retrieved May 31, 2007, from www.globalgreen.org/greenbuilding/GreenSchools.html.

Graziano, A. M., & Raulin, M. L. (2010). *Research methods: A process of inquiry*. Needham Heights, MA: Allyn & Bacon.

Greenberg, M. T. (2006). Promoting resilience in children and youth: Preventive interventions and their interface with science. *Annals of the New York Academy of Science*, 1094, 139–150.

Gunzelmann, B. (1998). A collective understanding of improving undergraduate psychology program and outcomes assessment. (Unpublished article).

Gunzelmann, B. (2004a). Doing good work with children: A meaningful workshop format for professionals. NHPA (Newsletter).

Gunzelmann, B. (2004b). Hidden dangers within our schools: What are these problems and how can we fix them? *Educational Horizons*, 83(1), 66–76.

Gunzelmann, B. (2005). Toxic testing: It's time to reflect upon our current testing practices. *Educational Horizons*, 83(3), 212–220.

Gunzelmann, B. (2008). Hidden problems in failing schools. *Educational Horizons*, 86(2), 85–97.

Gunzelmann, B. (2008, 2011). *Hidden dangers: Subtle signs of failing schools*. Lanham, MD: Rowman & Littlefield. (2nd edition in production).

Gunzelmann, B. (Fall, 2009). New era/new possibilities: Research-based education for equality and excellence. *Educational Horizons*, 88(1), 21–27.

Gunzelmann, B. (2010, 2011). *Hidden dangers to kids learning: Parent guide to cope with educational roadblocks*. Lanham, MD: Rowman & Littlefield Education. (2nd edition in production).

Gunzelmann, B. (2012). *Barriers to excellence: The changes needed for our schools*. Lanham, MD: Rowman & Littlefield Education.

Gunzelmann, B. (2013). *Global voices and global visions: Education for excellence, understanding, peace and sustainability*. Lanham, MD: Rowman & Littlefield Education.

Gunzelmann, B., and Connell, D. (2006). The new gender gap: Social, psychological, and educational perspectives. *Educational Horizons*, 84(2), 94–101.

Hansen, J. M., and Childs, J. (1998). Creating a school where people like to be: Realizing a positive school climate. *Educational Leadership*, 56(1), 14–17.

Harvard University, Civil Rights Project. (2001). Opportunities suspended: The devastating consequences of zero tolerance and school discipline. Retrieved May 30, 2007, from www.civilrightsproject.harvard.edu/convenings/zerotolerance/synopsis.php.

Harvard University, Civil Rights Project. (2003). Minority children with disabilities will be harmed in disproportionate numbers if IDEA's discipline safeguards are reduced or eliminated. Retrieved May 30, 2007, from www.civilrightsproject.harvard.edu/policy/alerts/idea.php.

Hokayem, C., and Heggeness, M. L. (May 2014). Living in near poverty in the United States: 1966–2012. Retrieved July 27, 2014, from https://www.census.gov/prod/2014pubs/p60-248.pdf.

Holzer, H. J., Schanzenbach, D. W., Duncan, G. J., and Ludwig, J. (January 24, 2007). The economic costs of poverty in the United States: Subsequent effects of children growing up poor. Retrieved July 27, 2014, from http://www.npc.umich.edu/publications/u/working_paper07-04.pdf.

Homeland Security Act, 2002.

Homeland Security National Preparedness Task Force (2006) Civil Defense and Homeland Security: A Short History of National Preparedness Efforts. DEPARTMENT OF HOMELAND SECURITY, Washington, DC.

Hoy, W. R., Tarter, C. J., and Kottkamp, R. B. (1991). *Open schools/healthy schools: Measuring organizational climate*. Newbury Park, CA: Sage.

Hoy, W. K., and Woolfolk, A. E. (1993). Teacher's sense of efficacy and the organizational health of schools. *The Elementary School Journal*, 93(4), 355–372.

Jackson, D. B. (April 2003). Education reforms as if student agency mattered: Academic microcultures and student identity. *Phi Delta Kappan*, 84(8), 658–664.

Jacobson, G., Riesch, S. K., Temkin, B. M., Kedrowski, K. M., and Kluba, N. (2014). School violence, role of the school nurse in prevention: Position statement. *NASN School Nurse* 29, 154–156.

Kids Health. (August 2005). Coping with cliques. Retrieved May 18, 2007, from www.kidshealth.org/teen/your mind/problems/cliques.html.

Kids Health. (June 2006). Lead poisoning. Retrieved July 15, 2007, from www.kidshealth.org/parent/medical/brain/lead_poisioning.html.

Kinscherff, R. December 2013, p. 3, *New England Psychologists.*

Kohn, A. (2004). Safety from the inside out: Rethinking traditional approaches. *Educational Horizons*, 83(1), 83–41.

Kozol, J. (2003). Speech at Duke University. Retrieved May 31, 2011, from http://today.duke.edu/2003/10/kozol1016.html.

Kozol, J. (1991). *Savage inequalities.* New York: Crown.

Mandela, N. (2002). In World report on violence and health: summary. Geneva, World Health Organization, 2002.

Mash, E. J. & Wolfe, D. A. (2013, Fifth Edition). *Abnormal Psychology.* Belmont, CA: Wadsworth Cengage Learning.

Maslow, A. H. (1959). *New Knowledge in Human Values*, New York, Harper.

Maslow, A. H. (1954). *Motivation and Personality*, New, York: Harper & Row.

McEvoy, A., and Welker, R. (2000). Antisocial behavior, academic failure, and school climate: A critical review. *Journal of Emotional and Behavioral Disorders*, 8(3), 130.

Meier, D. (2004). For safety's sake. *Educational Horizons*, 83(1), 55–60.

Merrow, J. (2004). Safety and excellence. *Educational Horizons*, 83(1), 19–32.

Moore, E. A. (2011). One week playing violent video games alters brain activity. Retrieved February 27, 2013, from http://news cnet.com.

National Center for Educational Statistics. (2012). Indicators of School Crime and Safety: 2012. Retrieved July 24, 2014, from http://nces.ed.gov/programs/crimeindicators/crimeindicators2013/key.asp.

National Center for Educational Statistics. (2013). Indicators of School Crime and Violence: 2013. Retrieved July 24, 2014, from http://nces.ed.gov/programs/crimeindicators/crimeindicators2013/index.asp.

National Center for Educational Statistics. (2007). Indicators of School Crime and Safety: 2007. Retrieved April 22, 2010, from http://nces.ed.gov/programs/crimeindicators/crimeindicators2007/.

National Clearinghouse for Educational Facilities. (2007a). Resource lists: Mold in schools. Retrieved May 20, 2007, from www.edfacilities.org/rl/Mold.cfm.

National Clearinghouse for Educational Facilities. (2007b). Resource lists: School cleaning and maintenance practices. Retrieved May 20, 2007, from www.edfacilities.org/rl/cleaning.cfm.

National Coalition for the Homeless, 2009.

National Conference of State Legislatures. Retrieved June 16, 2014, from http://www.ncsl.org/research/human-services/homeless-and-runaway-youth.aspx#_ednref1.

National Institute of Environmental Health Services. (May 2006). Asthma and its environmental triggers. Retrieved May 30, 2007, from www.niehs.nih.gov/oc/factsheets/pdf/asthma.pdf.

Obama, B. (February 2009). Press conference: National Coalition for Homeless Children. Retrieved June 15, 2014, from www.nationalhomeless.org/factsheets/families.

Patel, V., Ramasundarahettige, C., Vijayakumar, L., Thankur, J. S., Gajalakshmi, V., Gururaj, G., Suraweera,W., Jha, P., and Million Death Study Collaborators. (2012). Suicide mortality in India: A nationally representative survey. *Lancet*, 379(9834), 2343–2351.

Peterson, R. L., and Skiba, R. (2001). Creating school climates that prevent school violence. *Clearinghouse*, 74(3), 155–163.

Pollack, W. (1998). *Real Boys: Rescuing our sons from the myth of boyhood.* NY: Holt. (Pollack, 1998).

Pollack, W. S. (January 2010). Presentation at L&B Safe & Emotionally Supportive School Climates: Creating Healthy Connection.

Ratey, J. J. (2008). *Spark: The revolutionary new science of exercise and the brain.* New York: Little Brown and Co.

Ristuccia, J. M. (2010). Helping traumatized children learn. Presentation at School Mental Health: Treating Students K-12, January 29–30, 2010, Boston, MA.

Robers, S., Zhang, J., Truman, J., & Snyder, T.D. (2012). Indicators of School Crime and Safety 2011 (NCES 2012-002/NCJ236021). National Center for Education Statistics, .U.S. Department of Education, and Bureau of Justice Statistics, Office of Justice Programs, U.S. Department of Justice. Washington, DC.

Saltman, K. J., and Gabbard, D. (eds.) (2003). *Education as enforcement: The militarization in our schools*. New York: RoutledgeFalmer.

Santilli, J. (2002). Health effects of mold exposure in schools. *Current Allergy and Asthma Reports*, 2, 460–467.

Scott, K. A. (2008). *Violence prevention in low- and middle-income countries: Finding a place on the global agenda: Workshop summary: Board on Global Health Institute of Medicine, Kimberly A. Scott, Rapporteur*. Washington, DC: The National Academies Press.

Seligman, M. (1995). *The optimistic child: A revolutionary program to safeguard children from depression and build lifelong resilience*. New York: Houghton Mifflin.

Seligman, M. (1996). *The optimistic child*. New York: Perennial.

Seligman, M.A. (1990, 1998, 2006, 2011). *Learned optimism: How to change your mind and your life*. New York: Random House.

Seligman, M.A. (2007). *The optimistic child: A proven program to safeguard children against depression and build lifelong resilience*. New York: Houghton Mifflin.

Skiba, R. Reynolds, C. R., Graham, S., Sheras, P., Close Conoley, J., & Garcia-Vazquez, E. (2006) Are Zero Tolerance Policies Effective in the Schools? An Evidentiary Review and Recommendations. APA Zero Tolerance Task Force retrieved 12/13/14 from http://www.apa.org/pubs/info/reports/zero-tolerance.aspx

Stamm, J. (2007). *Bright from the start*. New York: Gotham Books.

Snyder, T., and Truman, J. (2012). Indicators of school crime and safety, 2012. Retrieved August 12, 2012, from http://www.bjs.gov/index.cfm?ty=pbdetail&iid=4677.

Taylor , S. J., & Bogdan, R. (1998). *Introduction to qualitative research methods: A guidebook and resource*. New York: Wiley.

Towey, K., and Fleming, M. (2006). *Policy and resource guide: Alcohol use and adolescents*. Chicago, IL: American College of Preventive Medicine and American Medical Association National Coalition for Adolescent Health.

U.S. Bureau of Census. (2010). Income, Poverty, and Health Insurance Coverage in the United States: 2010.

U.S. Department of Agriculture. (2013). Household Food Security in the United States in 2012. Economic Research Report No. (ERR-155). Retrieved July 26, 2014, from http://www.ers.usda.gov/publications/err-economic-research-report/err155.aspx#.U9P8gYBdXlR.

U.S. Department of Labor. (July 3, 2014) Statistics. Retrieved July 26, 2014, from http://www.bls.gov/news.release/empsit.nr0.htm.

U.S. Environmental Protection Agency. (March 1989). Recognition and management of pesticide poisonings. Retrieved May 20, 2007, from www.epa.gov/pesticides/safety/healthcare/handbook/handbook.pdf EPA 735–R-98–003.

U.S. Environmental Protection Agency. (June 1992). Healthy lawn, healthy environment. Retrieved May 20, 2007, from www.epa.gov/oppfead1/Publications/lawncare.pdf.

U.S. Environmental Protection Agency. (1994). *Reducing radon in the schools: A team approach* (EPA Report No. 402-R-94-008). Washington, DC: Author.

U.S. Environmental Protection Agency. (January 2002). Protecting children from pesticides. Retrieved May 20, 2007, from www.epa.gov/pesticides/factsheets/kidpesticide.htm.

U.S. Environmental Protection Agency. (2007a). Asbestos in schools. Retrieved May 20, 2007, from www.epa.gov/asbestos/pubs/schools.html.

U.S. Environmental Protection Agency. (2007b). Brownfields cleanup and redevelopment. Retrieved May 27, 2007, from www.epa.gov/swerosps/bf/.

U.S. Environmental Protection Agency. (2007c). Green indoor environments. Retrieved May 27, 2007, from www.epa.gov/iaq/greenbuilding/index.html.

U.S. Environmental Protection Agency. (2007d). High performance schools. Retrieved May 27, 2007, from www.epa.gov/iaq/schooldesign/highperformance.html.

U.S. Environmental Protection Agency. (2007e). Radon in schools (2nd ed.). Retrieved May 21, 2007, from www.epa.gov/radon/pubs/schoolrn.html.

U.S. General Accounting Office. (1996). Indoor air quality. School facilities: America's schools report differing conditions (GAO Report No. HEHS-96-103). Retrieved May 20, 2007, from www.gao.gov/archive/1996/he96103.pdf.

U.S. Secret Service and U.S. Department of Education. (2002, May). *The final report and findings of the safe school initiative: Implications for the prevention of school attacks in the United States.* Washington, DC: Author.

Weber (2005).

Welsh, W. (2000). The effects of school climate on school disorder. *Annals of American Academy of Political and Social Science,* 567, 88–107.

World Health Organization (2006). Facts on Alcohol and Violence: Youth Violence and Alcohol. Retrieved 12/15/14 from Retrieved 12/15/14 from http://www.who.int/violence_injury_prevention/violence/world_report/factsheets/fs_youth.pdf.

Willoughby, T., Adachi, P. J., and Good, M. (2012). A longitudinal study of the association between violent video game play and aggression among adolescents. *Developmental Psychology,* 48(4), 1044–1057.

Wolk, R. (2004). Thinking the unthinkable. *Educational Horizons,* 82(4), 268–283.

World Health Organization. (1992). *ICD-10: The classification of behavioral and mental disorders.* Geneva, Switzerland: Author.

World Health Organization. (2005). Child mental health atlas. Retrieved December 18, 2012, from http://www.who.int/mental_health/resources/Child_ado_atlas.pdf.